THE LANGUAGE OF THE BATON

By

ADOLF SCHMID

BOOK ONE

G. SCHIRMER, Inc.
New York

To the Memory

of

My Father

CONTENTS

CONTENTS

PREFACE

Conducting is an unspoken language. Its symbols, like musical tones themselves, are more profound, more direct, and more readily intelligible than spoken words. By means of these symbols, the man with the baton is able to conjure up the magic of music as a living art.

The magic of the baton's language rests upon no metaphysics, but rather upon a studied science which has probed deeply into the interpretation of musical compositions and which has subsequently evolved a fundamental system of clear and logical conducting motions. Simplicity and consistency are the keynotes of this system. The moment when conducting becomes complex and loses itself in a twisted labyrinth of movements and gestures, it defeats its own purpose. The conductor whose baton traces in the air intricate designs for Oriental rugs will produce only a blurred mass of rampant tone-color. Conducting motions, like the skills of the plastic arts, should make the composer's conception stand out in clean-cut contours.

The conductor, like every other artist, must possess such absolute command over fundamentals that technique becomes "second nature"—a reflex activity without any conscious exertion. When technique becomes utterly subservient to the interpretation of the composer's ideas, the conductor stands upon the threshold between music as a science and music as an art. The ultimate achievement of art depends upon the conductor's powers of interpretation, which must be perfected, within his spiritual and æsthetic powers, even before the baton is lifted.

In this book, the author has endeavored to present in practical and concise form the fundamental principles of conducting, without slighting those intangible qualities in music which must be psychologically comprehended. These principles, which are drawn from the analysis of representative musical examples and the accompanying diagrams, apply to conducting not only the orchestra, but also band and chorus, which employ the same technique.

The technique of the baton cannot be learned in "ten easy lessons". The student who seeks such charlatan short-cut methods will find it just as profitable, and certainly more enjoyable, to visit a ball-park and to watch the "baton" technique of the batter. In the process of becoming a good conductor, genius is not a requisite, but persevering work, high artistic ideals, and the benefits of actual conducting experience can never be minimized.

ACKNOWLEDGMENT

To Miss Anna Pfeifauf, who has given me invaluable assistance with the preparation of the text and diagrams for THE LANGUAGE OF THE BATON, I owe my most sincere gratitude.

New York City, July, 1937.

ADOLF SCHMID

CHAPTER I.

THE HISTORY OF THE BATON

The history of conducting extends back almost infinitely into the past of music. With the first instances of musical performance by more than one individual at the same time, arose the necessity for some means of keeping together. This necessity provided the stimulus for the evolving of certain systems to indicate the rhythmical pattern of the music played.

From the period of the ancient Egyptian and Greek choruses through the later ecclesiastical chants, the principal singer was the leader or the precentor, who established the tempo and the nuances and sang the solos in antiphonal music. The rhythm was probably stamped out audibly or marked by the strokes of the hand.

It was not until the fifteenth century that the *sol-fa*, the forerunner of the modern baton, came into use. The *sol-fa* was a paper roll, usually a part of the score. Documentary evidence reveals that it was used to direct the Sistine Choir at Rome. In the sixteenth century, the era of Palestrina and the greatest polyphonic music, the use of the *sol-fa* became the accepted manner of conducting.

After the development of instrumental music, purely vocal music became more and more confined to the Church. The advent of opera and ballet made instrumental music indispensable to every form of secular art and entertainment. A later development eventually made orchestral music entirely independent of the other arts.

The seventeenth century created the office and title of *Maestro di Cappèlla, Maestro di Canto, Maître de Musique, Chef d'Orchestre,* or *Kapellmeister* for the director of musical activities. The *sol-fa* was abandoned for the staff or cane whose audible tapping on the floor assisted the performances of the *Corps de Ballet* and the Chorus. Baroque pomp and resplendent vanity were manifested in the highly ornamental and gold betasseled staff of the conductor. Royal patrons probably took keen delight in insisting upon such an absurdity from the conductor, who had to cater to their whims. No doubt Louis XIV, whose favorite court composer and conductor was Lully, took particular pleasure in the grandiose manner in which his *Maître de Musique* paraded his magnificent staff. In this connection, we may recall the well-known report that Lully in 1687 is supposed to have misdirected a beat of his staff toward a gouty foot, whose subsequent amputation proved fatal.

It is of interest to know the odd manner in which the various tempos and rhythms were indicated by the staff or cane. Usually two audible taps on the floor and then one or more silent beats were counted to the bar. For example, in the $\frac{4}{4}$ rhythm, there were two audible and two silent beats. Both the $\frac{3}{4}$ and $\frac{6}{8}$ rhythms were marked by two taps and one silent beat. However, in the $\frac{2}{4}$ or $\frac{2}{2}$ (*alla breve*) rhythm, two taps were given only in the first of each four bars, and in each of the next three bars one audible and one silent beat alternated. This four-bar pattern was repeated to the end of the composition in a manner analogous to the present-day drum strokes for marches.

This style of conducting by tapping was also used by conductors who had to play an instrument at the same time. Obviously, they could not manipulate a bow and the staff simultaneously, so they sounded the taps with their feet. A vestige of this foot-tapping, incidentally, still survives in the method by which many performers today, notably jazz players, keep time.

Audible conducting was perhaps pardonable for martial or dance music, but it was most objectionable when the music was soft and gentle in character. For this reason, the staff was soon discarded and replaced by the Violin bow. Just as Lully first attained renown as a violinist and, in this capacity, eventually became a noted conductor, so orchestras in the eighteenth century were led by leading violinists or concertmasters, who played and conducted alternately.

Bach, Handel, Gluck, and Haydn are known to have played the Organ or Harpsichord while conducting performances. Solomon, the astute impresario, violinist, and concert director in London, placed Haydn "on display" by having the composer preside passively at the Harpsichord while he, himself, led the orchestra. Similar to this theatrical ostentation is the contemporary practice of exhibiting composers in a box or loge during the concerts and of afterwards vociferously coaxing them to the podium. When this type of "honoring" a composer and his work is scrutinized more discriminately, it will reduce itself to no more than box-office exploitation and an additional attraction for a sensation-seeking musical public.

Gradually instrumental music demanded additional resources and a greater number of players, a development which considerably increased the responsibilities of the conductor. Subsequently it became necessary for the conductor to relinquish his task as a performer and to devote his attention solely to conducting. A concomitant development was the change from the Violin bow to the baton, the stick, or the *Taktstock*.

The baton was not in active usage until the early nineteenth century when it was adopted and popularized by such composer-conductors as von Weber, Spohr, and Mendelssohn. The keen insight into interpretation granted to these men by their powers as composers made them the true pioneers of conducting as an art. The baton was liberated from its former position as a mere time-beater and became a highly sensitive and expressive instrument. Its vast interpretative capacities were revealed, and infinitely greater artistry was infused into conducting.

Within the scope of a few score years, the baton, as we know it today, has undergone many alterations. In length it has been decreased from as long as thirty inches to approximately eighteen inches, or less. The former gold ornamentation of inlaid ebony and ivory batons, usually the gifts of admiring monarchs and princes, has also disappeared. Franz Liszt, it might be mentioned, was on many occasions honored with these presentations, elaborate batons which have since become museum pieces.

As late as the twentieth century, Italian conductors frequently emphasized the tempo by tapping on the conductor's stand with the baton. Often the audience was irritated by this audible method of keeping the orchestra and stage performers together. Fortunately, the most modern usage has made the baton the instrument of communicating instantaneously and expressively in a dignified, entirely silent art, the intentions of the conductor.

CHAPTER II.

FUNDAMENTAL PRECEPTS OF CONDUCTING

To the conductor belongs the major responsibility for the successful performance of a musical work by a group of instrumentalists or singers—an orchestra, band, or chorus.

The conductor's chief activities may be outlined briefly in three units:

First: A thorough understanding of the composer's conception of the work as recorded in the score. A thorough interpretative knowledge of the work, including the correct tempos, phrasings, and dynamic effects.

Second: The rehearsing of the players or singers in their individual parts and in ensemble.

Third: The perfect interpretation of the work in public.

In directing an orchestra, band, or chorus, nearly every conductor employs a baton to indicate tempos, dynamics, and nuances. The expression, "to beat time", has purposely been avoided, since there is obviously a vast gulf between conducting and "time-beating".

The correct manner of holding the baton is that which affords the greatest ease, relaxation, and flexibility to the conducting strokes. The end of the baton should be gripped firmly—but never tensely—by the thumb and the second and third fingers. (*See Plates 3-7.*)

The manner of making baton strokes must be adjusted to the inherent qualities of the music played. Most of these strokes will be movements of the wrist and fore-arm. However, music of a forcible, broadly surging nature may at times require an appropriate larger movement of the entire arm from the shoulder. Quick marches and gallop movements will call into play decisive, angular, and sharply accentuated strokes of the baton, which will necessarily be comparatively small motions. For more graceful music, each stroke should describe a curving arc, and the baton should rebound easily from one position to the next of a distinct and intelligible rhythmical design. Each of these designs is based on a single bar of the music. It should be so easily and clearly understood that the players are never at a loss to recognize instantaneously the pulsation or the specific section of the design indicated by the stroke.

Some conductors prefer to direct without a baton and to make use of their hands only. Experience, however, proves this method to be satisfactory only for directing a small ensemble of instrumentalists or singers. Larger groups require a medium more visible than bare hands for guidance, because the hand movements of the conductor will be clearly discernible only to the performers in the foreground. The others will be able to see only the arm movements of the conductor and will find them difficult to observe because of the dark coat-sleeve material which further impairs the visibility. However, a baton, no matter how small, will be perceptible to everyone from all angles of the platform or pit.

In giving cues to the individual players, the baton will also be found superior to the bare hands, since it makes its direction felt more distinctly.

At a recent concert performance of an orchestra consisting of over two hundred players, one of our foremost American conductors, a man of international reputation, conducted without a baton. The difference between this performance with an orchestra strange to him and the performances with his own orchestra of about one hundred players was most marked. In spite of clear and masterful direction, there were a few perilous moments, during which disaster was prevented only by the conductor's wonderful presence of mind and the alertness of several highly experienced players. All of this uncertainty could be attributed to the absence of the baton. Although the orchestra members paid the closest attention and showed their joy in playing for the conductor, who gave every cue, it was difficult for them to follow his guidance without a distinctly visible point to be grasped by the eye.

The color, length, and weight of the baton are matters to be left to the conductor's discretion. For the sake of visibility, white is the preferable color for the baton.* It is advisable to use one of medium size and light wood to prevent straining the wrist and arm. Too long a baton will prove to be more of a hindrance than a help, particularly on a crowded platform. In spite of this fact, there are conductors who seem to believe that the larger the baton, the greater the conductor. Players rapidly accustom themselves to particular kinds of batons and the conductor will find the difference noticed if he deliberately or accidentally changes his customary baton.

The adeptness of players at sensing the difference in batons is illustrated by this little anecdote concerning Richard Strauss when he was a guest conductor at the Royal Opera in Vienna. In such a large opera house, there are often as many as five or six conductors, each of whom has his own type of baton, which is kept at the side of the conductor's desk. When Richard Strauss appeared, he had forgotten to give his own baton to the orchestra attendant to be placed on the stand. He did not miss his own baton until the moment of beginning the rehearsal. In order to avoid any delay, he selected a baton from one of those on the stand, but just as he gave the signal to begin, the principal Viola player stepped forward, courteously handed him another baton, and said, "Please, Master, take this one. The other has no rhythm. . . ."

---

*The prices of batons ordinarily range between 15 cents and $7.00.

Plate 1—TYPES OF BATONS

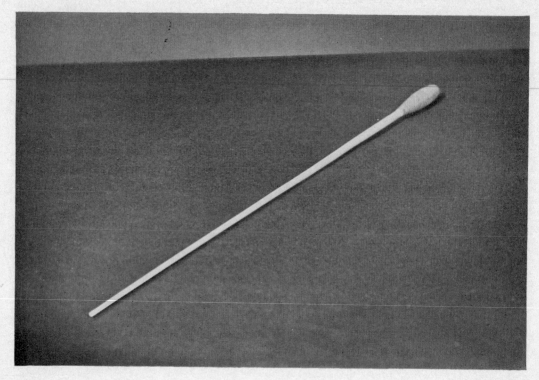

Plate 2

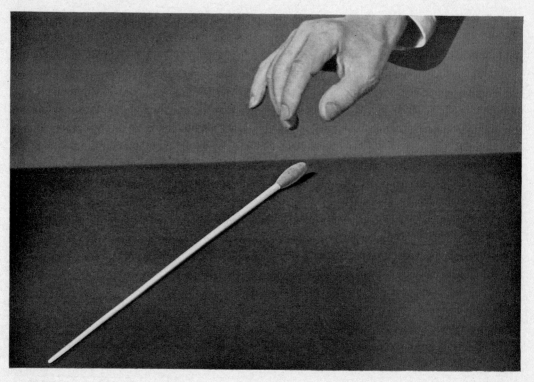

Plate 3

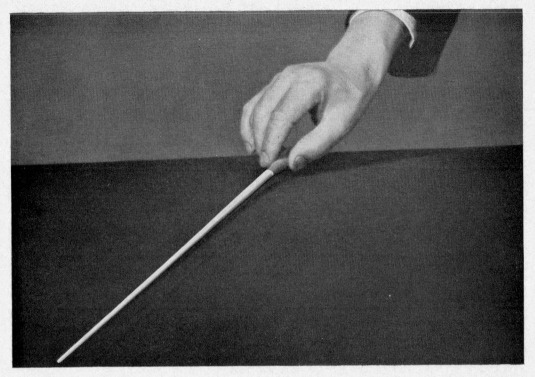

Plate 4

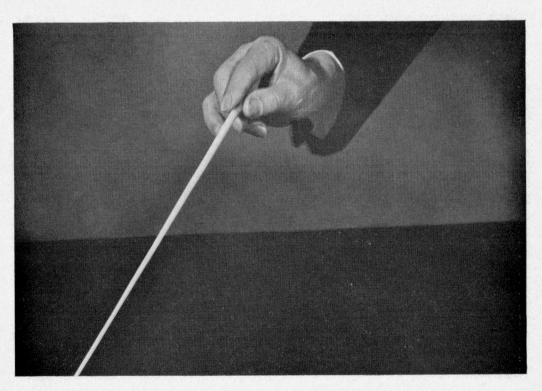

Plate 5

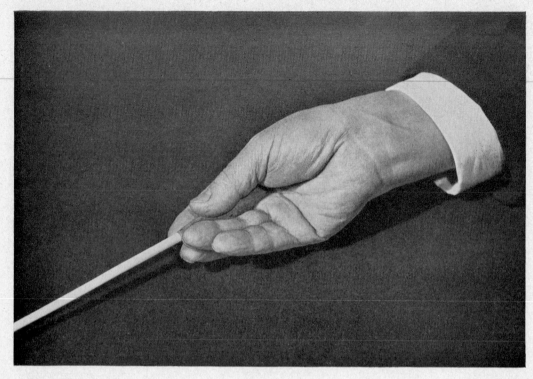

Plate 6

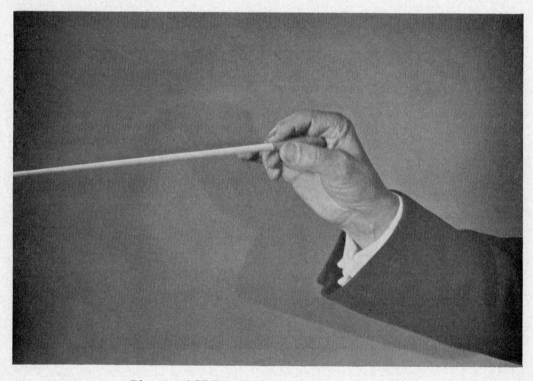

Plate 7—CORRECT GRASP OF THE BATON

CHAPTER III.

COORDINATION OF BATON AND LEFT HAND

The baton, when it is correctly handled, will reveal itself to be a most eloquent object, whose expressiveness by far surpasses that of the hands alone. The right hand with the baton should accomplish most of the work, while the left hand is free to support and to amplify the conductor's gestures. The left hand should be used only sparingly to emphasize certain tone gradations or changes in tempo.

Some conductors employ both hands practically all the time, a habit not to be encouraged for two reasons: First, the orchestra becomes so fixedly accustomed to the continual movement of both hands that changes in expression or rhythm will not be seen. Second, it is poor taste for a conductor to give the appearance of a cheer-leader on a college campus. When the right hand has been used for a considerable time and the left hand is taken up, the orchestra will notice at once the new motion. Attention has been attracted by a change, and it is quite natural for the players to follow the new movement.

As an example of the baton's coordination with the left hand, we shall consider the Prelude to "Die Meistersinger", which starts in the stately, majestic mood of a pompous march. To emphasize the forceful strength of the movement, the conductor will naturally begin by marking time with both hands. When the tempo and mood are firmly established after five or six bars, the conductor's left hand should retire and the baton alone should guide the tempos to the 14th bar. At this point, the *tutti fortissimo* for the re-entry of the principal motive should be emphasized by the conductor's taking up the left hand again and marking the movement with both hands for a number of bars. As soon as the full strength of the orchestra is established, the left hand may retire once more. There will be no need for it until the 26th bar where it will give the *diminuendo* sign for the entry of the second subject for Flute and Clarinet. This procedure may be applied throughout the Prelude.

In light, fanciful pieces, like the *Scherzo* from Mendelssohn's "Midsummer Night's Dream", it is entirely out of place to conduct with both hands. The baton alone should direct, while the left hand on very rare occasions gives the cue for the entry of a new instrument or the sign of a *diminuendo, sforzato, etc.* (*See Plate 10.*) When the conductor proceeds in this manner, he will find his baton transformed into a magician's wand, and the players will be unable to resist its enchantment.

Far more important than the left hand in conducting is the attention-compelling force of the conductor's eye. The conductor will remain calmly concentrated and will present a genuinely self-possessed appearance to his players and his audience. At the same time, he will be exercising a far stronger control than by gestures alone. Too many gestures become monotonous and meaningless to the players and irritating to the audience. To give cues for solo entrances or to players in the immediate vicinity of the conductor, only a nod of the head or a glance of the eye is necessary. The left hand will then be reserved for giving cues to groups of players, such as the Horns, Trumpets, Trombones, or to the whole section of Stringed or Wood-wind instruments.

CHAPTER IV.

SMOOTHNESS AND ACCENTUATION IN CONDUCTING

For the most part, the tempo should be given in a swinging motion, not in a jerky kind of movement. The motion of the baton should resemble the pendulum of a metronome without the ticking emphasis on the divisions of the bars. When it is used in this way, the pendulum-swing of the baton permits the melodic line to be fitted into the tempo without marking the actual accents of the sections in each bar.

The motion of conducting should at all times be an elastic one which will enable the players to observe more easily the exact marking of the tempo. (Musicians call this style of conducting "easy to follow", which is probably the greatest compliment they can pay to a conductor.)

However, the motion resembling a metronome's tick will at times have to be called into action for momentary emphasis on the tempo marking, particularly if the ensemble during rehearsal becomes uneven and requires a firm, accentuating force to re-establish itself. (It is understood that this "tick" of the baton is a matter of quality and shape of gesture, and in no way implies the actual sound of striking upon an object.)

To illustrate this point, if the opening measures of the *Andante con moto* of Beethoven's Fifth Symphony were to be practised on an instrument meticulously with the metronome, the result would be a jagged series of broken phrasings. The composer's idea, which is embodied in a smooth, melodic motive, would have been sacrificed. A similar result on a larger scale would be obtained from conducting an orchestra in such a precisely proportioned, mechanical way. However, at the 21st bar, where a rhythmically distinct, articulated pattern enters, the conductor will find the "ticking" motion most effective in lending a chiseled decisiveness to each tone. At the 29th bar, the entrance of the *fortissimo tutti* requires a strongly contrasted treatment. The majestic character of the heroic second theme is produced by the Wood-wind, Brass, Timpani, First Violins, 'Cellos, and Basses and by the accompanying rhythmical agitation of the triplet figure for Second Violins and Violas. To create this broad effect the conductor will necessarily amplify his movements until Bar 37, then decrease them again until the anacrusis of the 39th bar is reached. At this point, a *pianissimo* transition into the variation of the principal theme causes a reversion to a tranquil serenity carried out by abandoning the former extensive movements and allowing the baton to move smoothly and imperturbably in accord with the altered mood of the passage. A survey of the conducting during the first 97 bars of this movement will formulate a basic pattern for the performance of the remainder of the Second Movement.

In the *Scherzo*, a similar design of conducting is applicable, since its dynamic and rhythmical construction is almost identical with that of the former movement. The first eighteen bars, which include two *fermate*, are to be played quite smoothly without any accentuation. At the 19th bar *of the Scherzo*, the *fortissimo* entrance of the Horn motive, developing into a *tutti*, breaks into a decisively stamped-out rhythm. An analogous pulsating pattern from Bar 100 to the end of 140, carried out first by the Violins, is later taken up by the Wood-wind. At the *Trio*, the

6

robust motive of the *fugato* is constructed upon well-delineated triple accents continued throughout this section. At the 240th bar, the movement reverts to the initial gliding motion. The principal motive then appears in an entirely new *scherzando* mood in lightly ticking rhythm, which leads into the triumphant exuberance of the Final Movement.

Almost imperceptibly the rhythmical forces of the *Scherzo* have grown into the consummation of triumph in the Fourth Movement. The change of tempo from the *Scherzo* (*Allegro* $\d. = 96$) to the *Finale* (*Allegro* $\d = 84$; *alla breve*) is so slight as to be almost indistinguishable. The composer feels the infinite potentiality and pulsation of his idea growing constantly more powerful and transcendent until it rises to an exultant apotheosis. Additional exhilarating pulses are called into action. Instrumental voices which have been silent in the preceding movements are released. The orchestral resources are augmented by adding the Piccolo, Contra-bassoon, and three Trombones. The entire ensemble is caught up in a stirring martial movement, whose underlying rhythmical scheme is constructed as a continuation of the *Scherzo*. The conductor becomes a leader controlling a host of instruments surging forward toward the acme of triumphant achievement. He will require extraordinary skill and presence of mind to keep a firm grip on the reins which keep in check those unlimited forces which, if given their head, would run amuck and plunge disastrously into chaos, particularly in such passages as Bars 58 to 63 or Bars 130 to 150. At all times, the conductor must maintain his leadership and never allow himself to be swept on to destruction by the torrent of energy surging under his baton.

Turning back to the First Movement we see that the very kernel of the pulsating rhythm, which has characterized each successive movement, can be discovered in the initial four notes, termed the Fate Motive. (*See Pages 48-49.*) This particular subject, "Thus Fate knocks at the portal", is one of the most difficult passages for the conductor. After the four "knocks" have been distinctly sounded and the *fermata* has been taken off, a momentary pause ensues. The baton must then be raised briefly in the anticipation of the next decisive downstroke. Fundamentally the same rhythmical pattern to be found in this movement will be continued with occasional diversification in dynamics throughout all four movements. The tempo, *Allegro con brio* ($\d = 108$), sets the rhythmical criterion or the pulse of the entire work, which is one accent to the bar. The Horn entrance of the principal subject at Bar 59 and the second subject introduced by the First Violins at Bar 63 and resumed by the Clarinet and the Flutes, necessitates a relaxed, swaying motion in the conducting until the climax of the *tutti* is reached at the 94th bar. The conductor will have to be most observant in the succeeding passages, Bar 196 to 210, to secure good balance of tone. The two Horns playing in unison and the two Trumpets also in unison will tend to outweigh the timbre of the Wood-wind or Strings. In order to maintain a balance of harmony, the conductor will find it necessary to subdue the too prominent Horns and Trumpets and to bring out the tone of the Wood-wind. In the development of the *stretto* at Bar 440, the same principle holds true. If the Trumpets and Timpani are permitted to predominate, they will unbalance the effect of the reiteration with the Wood-wind and Strings.

In conclusion, it might not be amiss to call attention to the Fate Motive once more, since at times it seems to stand out as an interpretative "sore spot" in the conducting of the First Movement. Its correct interpretation remains, of course, a controversial problem. However, the fact can not be overlooked that Beethoven himself clearly indicated the tempo-marking according to the metronome. When the composer's intention in this respect is not deliberately slighted, a satisfactory result may be anticipated. Without doubt, Beethoven's conception was four emphatic "knocks" of Fate, an idea which has too often been distorted beyond recognition by the personal interpretations of conductors. Particularly during the last two decades such distorted conceptions have been prevalent in performances of the work. One conductor with much overdramatic, pompous display will attempt to shake the firmaments by heavily thundering forth four times. Another will attack the same four notes with the agile ferociousness of a leopard. Still another conductor vehemently hangs on to the last note with a suggestion of almost sinister premonition. Each of these conductors, one might say, is attempting to impress the audience with his own "genius" and to lead his listeners into believing that he alone has been able to discover the secret of Beethoven. Yet, if these self-appointed "discoverers" were sincere in their interpretations, they could perform the Fate Motive almost as easily as ringing a door-bell.

CHAPTER V.

GESTURES AND MANNERISMS

The conductor's arm movements should be confined to a reasonably small space. As far as possible, they should avoid exceeding the natural frame of the conductor's person.

The character of the music to be interpreted should be the chief factor determining the nature of the gestures. In other words, the composer, through his score, conveys to the conductor a network of emotions or a mood which provides the stimulus for shaping the arm movements. The ability to sense almost intuitively the composer's intentions and then to respond instantaneously with the most natural of gestures distinguishes the conductor from the robot.

Large movements of the baton should be used only for strong, forceful themes or motives. Light and easy motions should be reserved for lyrical, delicate, and gay themes. (*See Plate 11.*) It can readily be observed how incongruous an abrupt motion would be for conducting a *Berceuse*. Such a vigorous movement would utterly destroy the subdued tranquillity inherent in the *Berceuse*. It would be equally absurd and impossible to conduct a spirited Sousa March in a fashion adapted to the *Berceuse*.

In his analyses and interpretations, the conductor will have to rely to a large extent upon his own discretion in order to be expressive without placing undue emphasis where it is unnecessary and uncalled for by the composer.

Without overacting, the conductor will find facial expressions to be vital factors for communicating to the players the nuances of his interpretation. The conductor with the imperturbable "poker face", who never allows his thoughts to become visible for an instant, will be coldly received by both orchestra and audience. There remains, of course, the danger of permitting facial expression to degenerate into superfluous grimaces. The only profits of such superficiality will be repulsion and ridicule. A kind of harmonious trinity should exist among the conductor's facial expressions, his arm movements, and the mood of the music. The slightest gesture will then make itself felt at once and will cause an immediate response from the players.

Among choral directors, it has been observed how very often such facial mannerisms may detract from performances. During rehearsals it may be necessary to give visible suggestions for more articulate enunciation. However, such tactics should be eliminated entirely from the last few rehearsals and the public performance. The unmarred dignity of the finished presentation will thus add immeasurably to the actual greatness of the work.

Among conducting mannerisms to be avoided is also the pretentious practice of giving all of the cues all of the time. There are those affected conductors who strive to add luster to the semi-precious metal of their musicianship. They will with break-neck speed attempt cues for perhaps three Oboe notes and will then electrically snap to the Trumpet cue for a few sixteenth notes. The entire direction might have been indicated by a single sign to attract attention. Such "finicky" conducting deteriorates into a nervous succession of agitated fretting and head-wagging, all of which signifies nothing. It even defeats its own ulterior, hypocritical motive of impressing orchestra and audience with the fact that the

conductor is familiar with each cue and each note in the score.   For a conductor
to presume to give each cue is, therefore, not only impossible but also intolerable.

Naturally, much must be said in favor of the conductor's memorizing the
score.   However, it becomes an entirely different situation when he conducts
without the score.   This practice, to a large extent, must be considered a fad
and an undesirable mannerism.   The prerogative of conducting from memory
may be left to a few outstanding conductors, but not to their petty imitators.   At
the same time, conducting with or without a score is not to be considered as any
criterion by which performances may be judged.   The conductor who uses a
score may achieve just as great results as the one who uses none—and frequently
greater.

Conducting from memory often proves to be the means of undermining the
orchestra members' security and confidence in themselves and their leader.   Some
slip-up, such as the false entrance of a player, may have come about through a
misunderstood or an incorrect cue.   The absence of the score in this predicament
would make it extremely difficult to restore a balanced ensemble.   Such incidents
are less apt to occur with the conductor who supplements his memory with the
score and constantly reads and thinks several bars ahead of those being played.

For choir directors, it has become the accepted custom to conduct from
memory *a cappella* choruses.   However, it is the practice to use the score for
larger works with orchestral, Piano, or Organ accompaniment, such as cantatas,
oratorios, and operas.   But it must be repeated that whether or not the score
has been used is of no significance in evaluating the final artistic achievement.
Often the immodest conductor, who takes false pride in the retentiveness of his
memory, is in reality an automaton mechanically counting out bars and pauses,
and neglecting entirely the living import of the composer's inspired message.
Conceit and the desire for personal recognition cause the conductor to attract the
audience's attention away from the music to himself and his trivial personality.

Frantic gesticulation, unnecessarily violent waving of the arms, or any
other eccentric mannerism will prove to be decidedly detrimental to any performance and should be outlawed entirely from good conducting.   No amount of
rationalization can justify the conductor's transforming himself into a shadow-
boxer, an inexpert contortionist, or the master-of-ceremonies at a side-show.

The intelligent and discriminating student of conducting will be able to
benefit inestimably from a close observation of all types of conducting.   Paradoxically, he will learn just as much from analyzing exceedingly poor conductors
as from unusually good ones.   Such observations will equip the student with the
measuring rod of self-criticism.   He will practice conducting as though he stood
before a highly reflective mirror.   No movement will be concealed and every
gesture will be submitted at once for the approval or condemnation of the student's
own acute critical faculties.

The following anecdote about the eight-year old Mozart may serve to illustrate this thought.   The boy-composer, who had just made his first attempt at
writing a symphony, had been left to his own amusement in the house one day
while his parents and older sister, Marianne, paid a nearby visit.   About two
hours had elapsed before the family's return.   As they approached the house
entrance, they became aware of a most unnatural stillness about the place.

Ordinarily, they would have expected to hear Wolfgang's joyous laughter at play or the sound of his practising the Harpsichord or the Violin, both of which he played masterfully. As they entered the hall, they heard the stillness broken by a series of light tappings, then the sound of the boy's mumbling several indistinct phrases underneath his breath. Then, suddenly: "You fool! Why don't you play your instrument as I conduct? Now we must begin over again!" The previous silence and this sudden exhortation were explained when the parents and sister noiselessly opened the door to his bedroom. There was Wolfgang with the score of his symphony on a chair before him, while the orchestral parts were spread out in order on the bed. He had been mentally conducting his symphony and was now berating an imaginary Bassoon-player for an inaccuracy. Just as he had observed his father conducting the cathedral choir or orchestral concerts, so the boy with his own symphony imitated what he had seen. Not a note of his own composition was audible, but yet he conducted and heard every sound as distinctly as though he were leading a real orchestra.

Further inferences about the mental process connected with conducting may be drawn. It is frequently suggested that students listen to the radio or gramophone for the purpose of mastering conducting. This practice may be a very beneficial one, as long as it is limited to listening only, or to following the deviations in phrasing and tempo, particularly the much misused *tempo rubato*. But the actual conducting movements should under no circumstances be attempted at this time. In fact, they would be just as out of place and worthless as to attend a symphony concert for the purpose of pedantically aping each movement of the conductor. The net additions to the student's knowledge would, of course, be nil. It is therefore advisable for the student to cultivate as highly as possible the art of mental conducting and reflection before proceeding to the actual technique.

CHAPTER VI.

UNIFORM AND IRREGULAR PHRASINGS

To secure an even, well-balanced performance, it is necessary for the orchestra, either *tutti* or a few instruments, to attack the first note unanimously on either a down- or an up-stroke. A careless beginning and the ragged release of a *fermata* or final chord, either *ff* or *pp,* will be fatal to an otherwise good performance.

Furthermore, it is necessary that the conductor insist on uniform phrasing in all sections of the orchestra. For example, the First Violins must observe the same type of bowing: *legato, staccato, spiccato, saltando, etc.* Not only must the up and down bowings be simultaneous, but all First Violins should play on the same string and in the same position, since changing to other strings or varying the positions results in distinctly different tone-qualities. This practice should be the rule for Second Violins, Violas, 'Cellos, and Basses also. When the conductor demands this uniformity, the Strings will sound like one voice. If the players are left to their own devices in this matter, the conductor will find each player using a different style of bowing or position and thereby causing an unclear effect. Strict adherence to uniformity will give the String Section a brilliant and wholesome tone like a choir of human voices who observe their breath-taking at definite and simultaneous intervals.

Irregular bowings, however, may be legitimately and advantageously applied to produce *crescendo* or *diminuendo* effects in long sustained notes. In a large group of Strings, an increase in tone strength would ordinarily be interrupted at the change of the bows if the same bowings were being used by all the players. Irregular bowings in this case make the changes in individual bowings unnoticed and produce a continuous flow of increasing or decreasing tone.

The same principle of irregularity may also be applied to choral singing. Long sustained *crescendos* or *diminuendos* can only be produced by each individual singer's breathing according to his own capacity.

In the Wood-wind and Brass Sections, it is equally important to observe unanimous phrasings and breathings except for such special effects.

Composers should take particular care to consider the varying potentialities of the diverse instruments. But only too frequently scores may be found written in the medium of Piano phrasings. On the Piano, long *legato* passages are often extended over numerous bars, which, for this instrument, are the accepted and natural phrasings. However, these same passages performed in the orchestra will be found either impossible to play or ineffective. In these cases, the conductor will have to rely upon his ideas of interpretation and make the necessary adjustments in phrasing for the Strings, Wood-wind, or Brass. Irregular breathings must be discreetly handled by the players themselves in the Wood-wind and Brass Sections. Breaths must be taken wherever necessary, but without loss in strength of tone.

If the conductor is not a performer on a stringed instrument, or has no practical experience with Wood-wind or Brass instruments, he would find it of inestimable value to discuss the technicalities of phrasing with the principal players of the different orchestral sections. Such friendly discussions and exchanges of expert experience will greatly aid in the creation of an unanimously accepted idea, leading to the successful achievement of the work in question.

CHAPTER VII.

THE CONDUCT OF REHEARSALS

In order to achieve the best possible interpretation of a work, the conductor must analyze and study a score so well that he is familiar with each minute detail of it almost by memory. In this way, he will gain the respect and admiration of the musicians whom he leads, and he will minimize their mental and physical efforts in following his clear, authoritative directions. Rehearsing will be transformed from hard work into candid enjoyment. Much time and trouble will be spared. Enthusiasm and genuine pleasure will mark the anticipation of future rehearsals.

During rehearsals, the conductor should give his instructions in very few, but well-chosen, definite statements. Long, tedious explanations often create boredom and restlessness among those players not directly concerned with the instructions given at the moment.

To avoid inattention or unrest at the rehearsals, the conductor should keep his players interested constantly. If it is necessary to rehearse certain passages of a work in sections, the conductor should not devote too long a time to one group. On the contrary, he should direct his attention quickly from one group to another. In doing so, the group which has already been rehearsed gains time to "absorb" the instructions received. After each group has been given its turn, he may return to the first group, and so on, until the entire ensemble is ready to rehearse the particular phrase together.

The full attention of the players or singers must be demanded by the conductor at all times, whether at rehearsals or concerts. Conversations should be restricted. In order to gain successful discipline, the conductor must be dignified and serious in his work. He may be friendly, but never unduly familiar with those whom he directs. He never condescends to become the obtrusive busybody, rushing about from place to place, giving a little advice here, or stopping to tell a funny story there. The players must at all times feel that the conductor is their teacher, their leader, and their master.

It will require patience, confidence, and courage for the conductor to set personally a worthy example in every respect, including that of discipline. Good discipline implies no barrack-room or police-court hardening of the character through blind obedience to externally imposed codes. Such rigid tactics applied to musical organizations produce harsh, inflexible drillmasters, not conductors. The conductor must govern himself with that intangible controlling force which is born of a firm ethical character and self-respect.

Work during rehearsals will require of the conductor great alertness, tact, justice, endurance, and a sense of humor. If he cultivates these attributes, which might even be termed virtues, the conductor will find it easy to gain satisfactory results. On the other hand, indolence, impatience, or sarcasm are the most potent forces to poison or kill the good-will and enthusiasm of any orchestra or chorus, even the very best one.

One might say: "As the conductor, so the orchestra". The conductor who is prompt, alert, and accurate in his work will have no difficulty in demanding the same qualities from his co-workers. The conductor who is negligent in these matters may never hope to lead more than a mediocre group of slip-shod, inefficient players.

At rehearsals, it will be advantageous to everyone concerned if the conductor insists that each musician be in his place at least ten minutes prior to the appointed time. This interval is to be used for "warming-up", or the tuning of instruments and preliminary practice of difficult passages of the music to be rehearsed.

For tuning purposes, the correct pitch should be ascertained from a tuning-fork accessible to every instrumentalist. The principal players in each instrumental section should be responsible for the correct tuning of the instruments in their respective groups. The Concertmaster should take the correct pitch from the tuning-fork and then pass it on to the entire String Section. The first Oboe or Clarinet should perform the same duty for the Wood-wind, and the first Trumpet should attend to the Brass. It would not be amiss for the Timpanist to keep an ear alert to the Percussion Section.

At the appointed time, the conductor should take his place on the stand. With a minimum of preliminary talk, he should verify the correct pitch of the instruments and proceed at once with the rehearsal.

CHAPTER VIII.

BATON TECHNIQUE AND DIAGRAMS

The basis for attaining perfection in conducting, just as in any of the other arts, must be technique. As its Greek derivation connotes, technique is the means of achieving actual artistry. It must be developed to such a high degree as to become independent of all conscious mental exertion.

Fluency, ease, and, above all, natural grace should mark the well developed technique of conducting movements. Practice and more practice will be the only means of attaining this end. Just as painstakingly and perseveringly as the instrumentalist or the singer must practise in order to gain absolute mastery of his technique, so the conductor must continuously practise each stroke of the baton until every conceivable technical difficulty has been overcome. Technique must be perfected until it becomes an unobtrusive reflex activity, which at all times is utterly subordinate to the demands of interpretative art. When this level of mastery has been reached, the conductor's conception of a work will be free to grow under his baton into a satisfying artistic performance with a precision and propriety of tempo, dynamics, attacks, and releases.

Each gesture of the conductor must necessarily be simple and unequivocal, in order to be understood instantly by the players. For the same purpose, the strokes of the baton must be constructed according to definite designs which possess the utmost clarity and consistency. These designs, the fundamental principles of conducting technique, are based on the geometric figure underlying the particular hand motion which is most natural to a given rhythm.

The chief figures are:

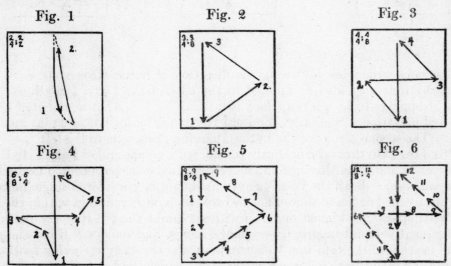

Fig. 1   Fig. 2   Fig. 3

Fig. 4   Fig. 5   Fig. 6

A brief analysis of these figures, which common usage has standardized, will reveal several generally accepted principles true of all baton strokes:

(1) The strongest pulsation of the bar is usually emphasized by a downward motion of the baton.

15

(2)   The successive strokes are usually weaker in pulsation and lead to an upward motion completing the figure.

(3)   In all even rhythms ($\frac{2}{4}$; $\frac{4}{4}$; $\frac{6}{8}$; $\frac{12}{8}$), the second stroke moves to the left. Conversely, in the uneven rhythms ($\frac{3}{4}$; $\frac{9}{8}$), the direction of the second stroke is towards the right of the conductor.

In the old conducting method which was used particularly by the Italian school and which unfortunately is not entirely obsolete today, the second stroke moved to the left for all rhythms. However, the practicability and clarity of such conducting strokes may be seriously questioned, especially in modern music where frequently alternating rhythmical changes occur. For this reason, the practice which has become almost universally accepted today clearly differentiates between even and uneven rhythms by diametrically opposed second strokes.

The rhythmical figures which are less frequently encountered are the following:

Fig. 7.   Fig. 8.   Fig. 9.

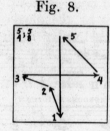 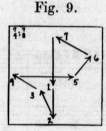

The same principles governing the direction of baton strokes for even and uneven rhythms may also be applied in the case of the $\frac{5}{4}$ and $\frac{7}{4}$ rhythms. Although it appears to be uneven, the $\frac{5}{4}$ is in reality a $\frac{4}{4}$ rhythm augmented by an additional pulsation. Similarly, the $\frac{7}{4}$ or $\frac{7}{8}$ rhythm is basically $\frac{6}{4}$ or $\frac{6}{8}$ plus an extra stroke. The second stroke of the baton, therefore, proceeds to the left.

Often the $\frac{5}{4}$ rhythm is erroneously considered a compound of $\frac{3}{4}$ and $\frac{2}{4}$ rhythms, or vice versa, and is on this account played with false accentuation uncalled for by the composer. Both the $\frac{5}{4}$ and $\frac{7}{4}$ rhythms should be considered single metrical units, just as the $\frac{3}{4}$ or $\frac{4}{4}$, and should not be broken up into groupings within the bar.

The simplest rhythmical meter is without doubt the $\frac{2}{4}$. It is the pulsation most frequently found in primitive chants, songs, and dances. Hand-clapping and the beating of the tom-tom to accompany the regularly recurring footfall in marching or dancing both follow a $\frac{2}{4}$ pattern from which the $\frac{3}{4}$ and all other rhythms were subsequently evolved.

The geometric diagrams already presented represent only the bare skeletons of the actual baton movements. They set forth the rudimentary structure of the pattern for each rhythm, which remains fundamentally unaltered, regardless of tempo, slow or fast. In practice, decidedly angular motions are applicable only for *staccato* effects, as required, for example, in the following excerpts:

Ex. 1. *(See Fig. 1.)*
Ballet Music from "Rosamunde"*

Franz Schubert
(1797-1828)

Andantino (quasi allegretto)

*Eulenburg Miniature Score No. 817.

Ex. 2. *(See Fig. 2.)*
Carillon from "L'Arlésienne", Suite No. 1*

Georges Bizet
(1838-1875)

Allegretto moderato ♩. = 104

* Eulenburg 828.

Ex. 3. *(See Fig. 3.)*

Prelude from "L'Arlésienne", Suite No. 1*   Georges Bizet

Allegro deciso, Alla Marcia ♩ = 104

* Eulenburg 828.

Music which demands a smooth interpretation must be conducted with correspondingly smooth and curving strokes. The sharpness of the angles must be rounded off with unfaltering beauty of form. The following diagrams, which retain their fundamental direction, serve to illustrate the actual motions of the baton:

Fig. 10   Fig. 11   Fig. 12   Fig. 13

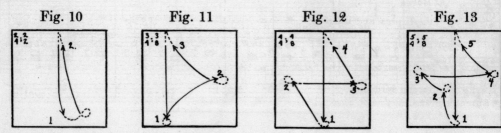

Fig. 14   Fig. 15   Fig. 16   Fig. 17

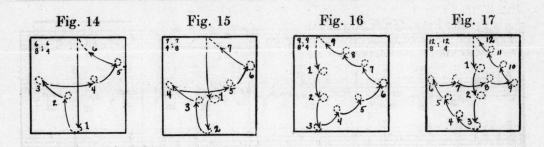

Musical examples to which the preceding diagrams may be applied are the following:

Ex. 4. *(See Fig. 10.)*
Entr'acte No. 2 from "Rosamunde"＊   Franz Schubert

＊Eulenburg 817.

Ex. 5. *(See Fig. 11.)*
Adagietto from "L'Arlésienne", Suite No. 1＊   Georges Bizet

＊Eulenburg 828.

Ex. 6. *(See Fig. 12.)*

The President's March, in
"From the Days of George Washington"*
Marziale, maestoso ♩ = 116

Arranged by
Adolf Schmid

*G. Schirmer, Inc.

Ex. 7. *(See Fig. 14.)*

Andantino from "L'Arlésienne," Suite No. 1*

Georges Bizet

Andantino ♩. = 54

* Eulenburg 828.

Experience in conducting slow tempos will bring out this general principle: the slower the music, the more curving and elaborate the baton movements become.   The movement of the baton naturally must become somewhat more extensive, since a simple stroke might incur "dragging" or pausing.   Each stroke must be enlarged with additional curving figuration, particularly in the frequently used $\frac{2}{4}$, $\frac{3}{4}$, and $\frac{4}{4}$ rhythms.   In the case of $\frac{5}{4}$, $\frac{6}{8}$, $\frac{7}{4}$, $\frac{9}{8}$, and $\frac{12}{8}$ rhythms, additional curves are seldom needed.

Diagrams of the baton strokes for slow tempos follow:

Fig. 18   Fig. 19   Fig. 20

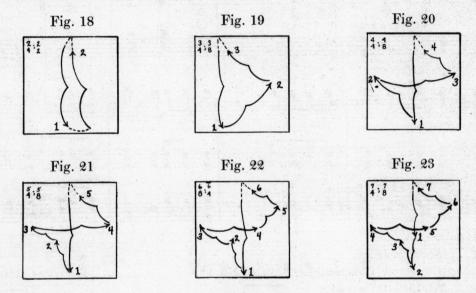

Fig. 21   Fig. 22   Fig. 23

Some conductors may wish to amplify the smoothness and breadth of the preceding baton movements by extending and completing the added curve in each stroke without changing the tempo.

Fig. 24   Fig. 25   Fig. 26

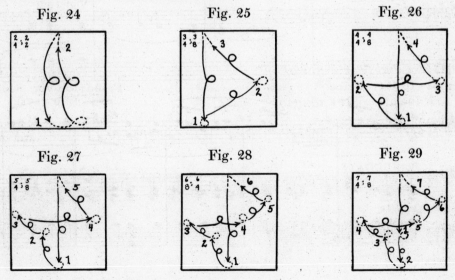

Fig. 27   Fig. 28   Fig. 29

Several musical examples in slow tempos follow:

Ex. 8. *(See Fig. 18 or Fig. 24.)*
Overture to "A Life for the Czar"＊
Adagio ma non tanto

Michael Glinka
(1803-1857)

＊Eulenburg 638.

Ex. 9. *(See Fig. 19 or Fig. 25.)*
Overture to "Stradella"＊
Andante quasi adagio

Friedrich von Flotow
(1812-1883)

*Eulenburg 679.

Ex. 10. *(See Fig. 20 or Fig. 26.)*

First Movement from Symphony in D Minor*   César Franck
                                                (1822–1890)

*Eulenburg 482.   By permission of J. Hamelle; Paris.

Often the rhythmical pulsation of musical passages must be clearly and precisely delineated by means of subdivision, or the dividing of each baton stroke into two sections. When it is discriminatingly applied, this rhythmical emphasis and articulation of detail adds immeasurably to the forward movement of the phrasing and the entire composition. At times, subdivision must be resorted to for the underlying rhythm of a phrase, while the *melos* retains its broad and flowing movement.

It is of primary importance that the use of subdivision should maintain the rhythmical accentuation indicated by the composer's marking. A subdivided $\frac{2}{4}$ rhythm must retain its characteristic $\frac{2}{4}$ pulsations. Except for very rare cases (see Example 40) usually occurring in very slow tempos, the substitution of a $\frac{4}{8}$ pattern in conducting a $\frac{2}{4}$ rhythm would distort the essential pulsations and would, therefore, misrepresent the composer's ideas.

As indicated by the light and dark shading of the subdivision diagram (Figs. 30-41) the conductor must take special care to make the first section of each stroke more emphatic than the second. This rhythmic device is absolutely essential for maintaining the fundamental pulsation of the *staccato* or *sostenuto* phrasings.

Diagrams and musical illustrations for *staccato* or *marcato* subdivisions follow:

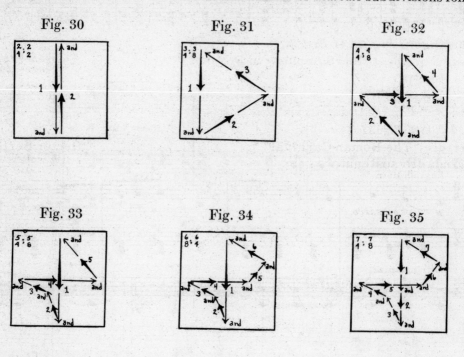

Fig. 30   Fig. 31   Fig. 32

Fig. 33   Fig. 34   Fig. 35

Ex. 11. *(See Fig. 30.)*
Ballet Music No. 2 from "Rosamunde"*   Franz Schubert

*Eulenburg 817.

Ex. 12. *(See Fig. 31.)*

Overture,"The Roman Carnival"*

Hector Berlioz
(1803-1869)

Andante sostenuto ♩ = 52

*Eulenburg 620.

Ex. 13. *(See Fig. 32.)* *

Overture to "Oberon" *

Adagio sostenuto

Carl Maria von Weber
(1786–1826)

* Eulenburg 607.

The subdivisions of *sostenuto* and expressive phrasings are illustrated by the following diagrams and musical excerpts:

Fig. 36   Fig. 37   Fig. 38

Fig. 39   Fig. 40   Fig. 41

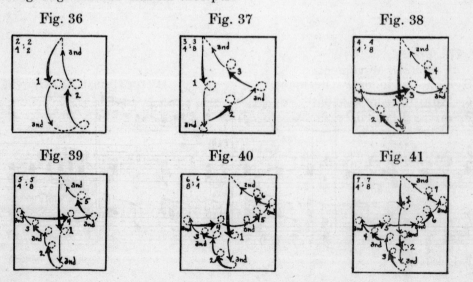

Ex. 14. *(See Fig. 36.)*
"Leise, leise, fromme Weise",
Aria from "Der Freischütz" *

Carl Maria von Weber

*G. Schirmer, Inc., Vocal Score, page 72.

Ex. 15. *(See Fig. 37.)*
Fourth Movement
of Symphony No. 6 ("Pathétique")*

Peter Ilyitch Tchaikovsky
(1840-1893)

*Eulenburg 479.

Ex. 16. *(See Fig. 38.)*
Prelude to "Parsifal"*   Richard Wagner
                                                        (1813-1883)
Adagio molto

*Eulenburg 666.

It must be remembered that all of the preceding musical examples (Ex. 1-16) are selected excerpts illustrating the application of only one specific type of baton movement. Obviously a complete composition will very rarely call for only one type of conducting method, since shadings in tone-color and skilful realization of rhythmic subtleties are dependent upon variation. The solution to these problems lies in the conductor's exhaustive interpretative analysis of the work, which will lead him to feel impulsively the type of conducting gesture which best lends itself to the shaping of certain passages and gains the desired effect.

CHAPTER IX

PREPARATORY BATON MOVEMENTS

No piece of music may be begun without some type of brief preliminary gesture. This is true not only of conducting, but in a larger sense applies also to the singer who prepares for the first tonal attack, or the player who performs on the Piano, the Violin, or any other instrument.

Before life is imparted to the first tone, the conductor must prove himself to be a master of psychological suggestion to the extent of infusing his own musical concept into the mind of every player under his leadership. Mere rapping with the baton on the conductor's stand is not sufficient to bring about this complete amalgamation and control of individual thought and will. The governing force must be the projection of the conductor's personality and the players' utter confidence in his incontrovertible musicianship. Not until the concentrated thought of the players is focused upon the conductor, and attention is at its highest point, should the composition actually be begun.

In order to secure a precise and unified attack, the first note of the composition must be anticipated by a clearly executed preparatory stroke. Whether this movement proceeds up or down or to the side is of no great consequence; but the fact remains that some type of preparatory gesture must be made. This stroke holds the responsibility of accurately communicating to the orchestra the tempo, the rhythm, the dynamics of the opening passage, and the character of the entire composition.

For establishing the correct tempo and rhythm, a supplementary preliminary signal may sometimes be advantageously employed. A small gesture of the raised left hand, or almost imperceptible but readily comprehended movements of the baton, may indicate the time, somewhat like the click of the metronome. For example, in a $\frac{2}{4}$ rhythm, the slight motion of one or two fingers of the left hand or the baton may be used to mark the pulsation of a complete bar, immediately before the preparatory baton stroke.

The dynamics of the composition will determine the manner in which the preliminary stroke is executed. In the *piano* movement, a small light motion will suffice, but a *fortissimo* opening tone will naturally require a much larger and more forceful stroke. (*See Plates 8 and 9.*)

It is essential to perform the preparatory stroke in keeping with the proper spirit of the music. The fact is self-evident that for a march the opening stroke is far different from that which is motivated by music of a contrastingly smooth and tranquil nature.

When a composition begins on the first and strongest pulse of a bar, the most practical direction for the preparatory movement is based on the position of the last stroke in an applicable metrical diagram. This principle may be observed in the following diagrams and musical examples, for which *the preparatory strokes are indicated in each case by the added dotted line.*

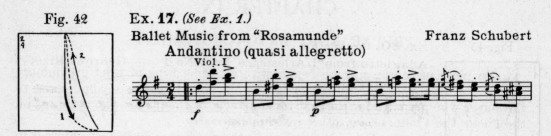

Fig. 42

Ex. **17.** *(See Ex. 1.)*
Ballet Music from "Rosamunde"   Franz Schubert
Andantino (quasi allegretto)

This excerpt calls for such a precise *forte* attack that in most cases it will be advisable to mark the rhythm with the almost imperceptible movement of the baton or the fingers of the left hand just before the preparatory stroke is made. In order to gain a rhythmically accurate and pulsing movement, the preparatory up-stroke and the first down-stroke of the $\frac{2}{4}$ rhythm will have to be performed almost simultaneously.

Fig. 43

Ex. **18.** *(See Ex. 2.)*
Carillon from "L'Arlésienne," Suite No. 1   Georges Bizet
Allegretto moderato ♩.= 104

In this case, the preparatory stroke is performed in the direction of the stroke for the third quarter of the bar, so that the first down-stroke can not be missed. The metronome marking (♩.= 104) calls for a rapid tempo, so that the up-stroke rises and falls into the first down-stroke without any additional pulsation which would break the rhythm. The proper accentuation will be obtained by conducting this type of rhythm as though there were but one heavy accent in each bar, even though there are three distinct pulsations.

Fig. 44

Ex. **19.** *(See Ex. 4.)*
Entr'acte No. 2 from "Rosamunde"   Franz Schubert
Andantino

The preliminary stroke, in this example, must forecast the lyricism and tranquillity of the mood, as well as indicate the even *andantino* tempo and the easy swing of the simple rhythmical figure.

Fig. 45

Ex. **20**. *(See Ex. 5.)*
Adagietto from "L'Arlésienne", Suite No. 1   Georges Bizet

The preparatory stroke for this excerpt is similar in many respects to that for the preceding example, although it must be performed more slowly and in keeping with the *adagio* tempo marking.

Fig. 46

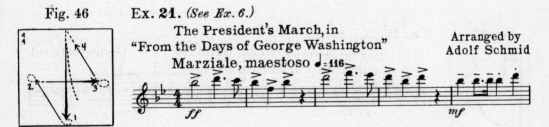

Ex. **21**. *(See Ex. 6.)*
The President's March, in
"From the Days of George Washington"   Arranged by
                         Adolf Schmid

This robust martial movement demands firmness and vigor of attack. Care must be taken to keep the preparatory stroke and each successive baton stroke in strict time within each metrical unit.

Fig. 47

Ex. **22**. *(See Ex. 7.)*
Andantino from "L'Arlésienne", Suite No. 1   Georges Bizet

Although this *andantino* is written in $\frac{6}{8}$ rhythm, the metronomic marking (♩.= 54) makes the pulsation distinctly a duple one. Each pulsation consists of a group of three notes, so that there are two accents to each bar. The time allotted to the up-stroke is, therefore, equivalent to the time value of a group of three notes.

Fig. 48   Ex. **23.** *(See Ex. 8.)*

Overture to "A Life for the Czar"   Michael Glinka

Adagio ma non tanto

This $\frac{2}{4}$ *adagio* should be introduced by a correspondingly slow and smooth preparatory movement, which must produce a similar spontaneous response from the orchestra. The additional curving figuration necessary to the general conducting scheme for the slowness of the tempo also applies, but in a lesser degree, to the up-stroke. During the pause in the 4th bar, the conducting movements continue but are reduced to unobtrusive small-scale proportions. The second pulsation in the pause constitutes another up-stroke similar to that for the first bar.

Fig. 49   Ex. **24.** *(See Ex. 9.)*

Overture to "Stradella"   Friedrich von Flotow

Andante quasi adagio

The same principles governing the preceding $\frac{2}{4}$ *adagio* excerpt are applicable to this $\frac{3}{4}$ *andante quasi adagio* movement.

Fig. 50   Ex. **25.** *(See Ex. 10.)*

First Movement from Symphony in D Minor   César Franck

Lento

As in Examples 24 and 25, the preparatory movement for this *Lento* excerpt has its origin in a hardly noticeable flex of the arm muscle, which is sufficient to communicate the pulsation to the players.

Fig. 51

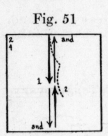

Ex. **26.** *(See Ex. 11.)*
Ballet Music No. 2 from "Rosamunde"   Franz Schubert

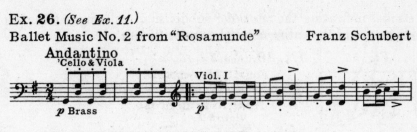

An additional impulse in the preparatory up-stroke suffices to introduce the short pulsations of a subdivided *staccato* rhythm which characterizes the entire movement.

Fig. 52

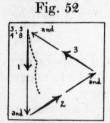

Ex. **27.** *(See Ex. 12.)*
Overture, "The Roman Carnival"   Hector Berlioz

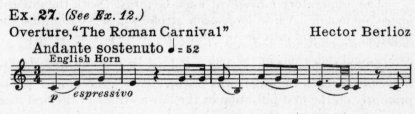

This excerpt presents the thread of the melodic line which, as may be observed in Example 12, is woven over a subdivided $\frac{3}{4}$ *pizzicato* rhythm in the Strings. This underlying rhythmical device is suggested by the up-stroke, without any unnecessary break in the melody.

Fig. 53

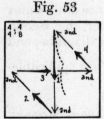

Ex. **28.** *See (Ex. 13.)*
Overture to "Oberon"   Carl Maria von Weber

The divided up-stroke must lead the way to a light *staccato* and *pianissimo* attack for the Trumpets, Horns, Bassoon, and later Strings.

Fig. 54.

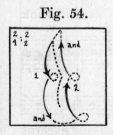

Ex. **29.** *See (Ex. 14.)*
"Leise, leise, fromme Weise",
Aria from "Der Freischütz"   Carl Maria von Weber

The slow and gentle curve of the preliminary baton movement should seem to blend into the perfect tranquillity of the melody. This lightly curving up-stroke, indicating the *sostenuto* subdivision, will suggest the expressiveness and eloquence of the entire musical composition.

Fig. 55

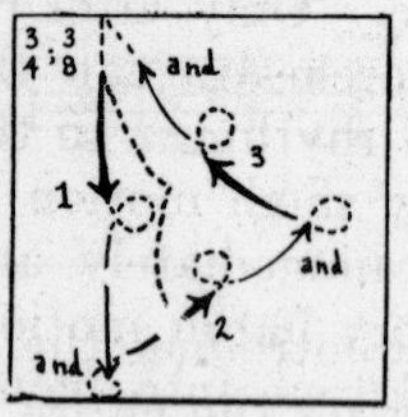

Ex. **30.** *See (Ex. 15.)*

Fourth Movement
of Symphony No.6("Pathétique")   Peter Ilyitch Tchaikovsky
Adagio lamentoso

The preparatory movement must be infused with the intensity of this *adagio lamentoso* mood.   A firm *largamente* stroke will serve to infuse the power and the depth of this mood into the opening *forte* tones of the Strings.

All of the foregoing musical examples (Ex. 17-30) have involved preparatory movements, each of which was an up-stroke preceding a phrase which began promptly on the first pulsation or the down-stroke of the first measure.

For measures beginning with an anacrusis, or a fractional part of a measure, the preparatory stroke will require adaptation to the individual case.   Except for rare instances, the anacrusis should not receive the heaviest accentuation. The emphatic stroke falls on the first pulse of the bar.   If this fact is overlooked, an entirely distorted rhythm will be produced.

In an anacrusis, for example, beginning with the second pulsation, the preparatory movement corresponds in direction, length, and time-value to the first baton stroke of an applicable diagram.   Similarly, if the measure begins with the third pulse, the preparatory movement is modeled after the second stroke of a diagram.   This principle is carried out in the following diagrams and musical examples:

Fig. 56

Ex. **31.**

Fourth Movement from
Symphony in G Minor*   Wolfgang Amadeus Mozart
Allegro assai   (1756-1791)

*Eulenburg 404.

The preliminary stroke preceding the anacrusis in the above example may be practically and correctly carried out in either one of two ways: First, the safest method of gaining an attack in unison is the raised left hand's marking two unostentatious pulsations; simultaneous with the second of these pulsations are the up-stroke of the baton and the first tone of the motive. Only after repeated rehearsals have established the correct tempo for the orchestra can the conductor afford to dispense with the left hand's signaling the rhythm. In the second method, a single pulsation may be indicated by a very small motion of the baton instead of the left hand. The up-stroke follows immediately and will have to be noticeably more emphatic than the preparatory baton motion, since the up-stroke now figuratively lifts the first orchestral tone into being. The conductor must take care to keep the preparatory stroke and each succeeding baton movement alive with the light *piano* vivacity which characterizes this movement.

Reference to the notation of Classical musical literature will serve to explain the *alla breve* time-signature in the above excerpt from the Fourth Movement of Mozart's Symphony in G Minor. The figure C in the signature denotes four crotchets for each measure. The divisional line ¢ then signifies that only two pulsations, instead of four, are to be allotted to each measure. These two will fall on the first and third quarters. In the old forms of notation, as also in modern usage, the *alla breve* was used to halve the time-value of each measure in order to quicken the tempo. But the fact may also be recalled that the old masters were not always precise in marking the divisional line to indicate specifically when the *alla breve*, or "cut time", was desired. Therefore the term or the sign led to unnecessary confusion. The ambiguity of the *alla breve* sign is causing it to become obsolete in modern notation. Instead, as a sure means of avoiding possible misunderstanding, contemporary composers are substituting $\frac{2}{2}$, a practical marking which promises to become universally adopted.

Fig. 57 Ex. **32.**

Third Movement
of Symphony in G Minor* Wolfgang Amadeus Mozart
Menuetto
Allegretto

*Eulenburg 404.

In this example, it will be advisable for the baton to give the second stroke of the diagram as a preparatory stroke. A similar motion in a reversed direction may also be made by the left hand. Each of the strokes for this *forte* attack will necessarily be strong and decidedly accentuated, without becoming unduly heavy.

Fig. 58

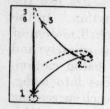

Ex. 33.

Second Movement of Symphony No. 5*

Andante con moto ♪ = 92

Ludwig van Beethoven
(1770-1827)

*Eulenburg 402.

The preparatory motion in this case is produced by a minute reflex of the arm muscle which serves to establish the characteristic rhythmical pattern taken up first by Viola and 'Cello and later by other instruments in the course of the Second Movement. Above all, it is important in this work to observe the metronomic marking (♪ = 92) indicated by Beethoven. Under no circumstances should the work be hurried along to an unsatisfactory conclusion. The left hand should at the outset follow in reverse each motion of the baton, as an additional visual aid for maintaining the rather slow *andante* movement.

Fig. 59

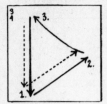

Ex. 34.

Minuetto from "L'Arlésienne", Suite No. 1*   Georges Bizet

Allegro giocoso ♩ = 184

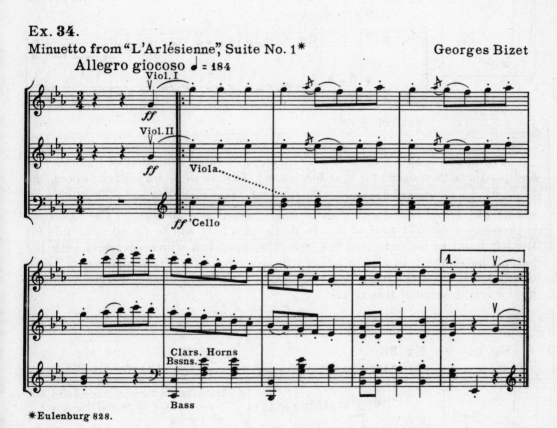

*Eulenburg 828.

The light, joyous exuberance of this *Minuetto* demands a very fast tempo, as indicated by the metronomic marking(♩ = 184). At the beginning, Bizet carefully wrote two quarter rests. These exact markings were made by the composer in order to ensure the precision of the initial attack. The two rests may be correctly looked upon as indicating preparatory movements. The first motion of the baton is a light down-stroke applied to the first silent pulsation or rest. The second stroke of the diagram follows, for the second rest, and leads without a break into the third stroke whose impulsive strength gains a *fortissimo* attack of the Strings. Conducting the entire measure in this manner is of particularly valuable assistance to those instrumentalists who must count the bars preceding their entries. If no rests whatsoever had been marked before the anacrusis, a preparatory movement in the position of the second baton stroke would have been necessary to gain a unified attack.

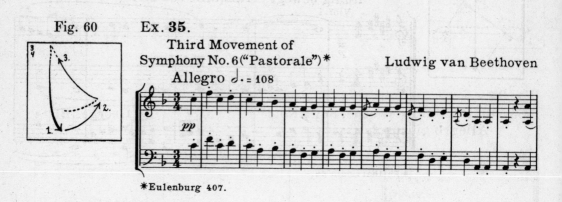

Fig. 60

Ex. **35**.

Third Movement of
Symphony No. 6("Pastorale")*   Ludwig van Beethoven
Allegro ♩. = 108

*Eulenburg 407.

The tempo in this *Scherzo* is very much more rapid than that of Example 34, and produces the effect of a fleet foot-race. There can be no mistake about the tempo because the metronomic marking (♩. = 108) necessitates a rhythm consisting of a triple figure with only a single accent per measure. The anacrusis is therefore a distinct part of this triple rhythm. It will be found advisable for the left hand to indicate two full bars, the second of which coincides with the baton's up-stroke. In such a quick tempo it would be very dangerous to begin this composition with only a single up-stroke of the right hand. Precision should be the very essence of this attack.

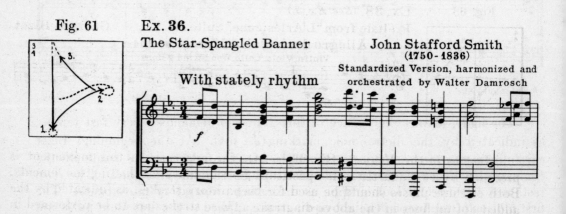

Fig. 61

Ex. **36**.
The Star-Spangled Banner   John Stafford Smith
(1750-1836)
Standardized Version, harmonized and
orchestrated by Walter Damrosch
With stately rhythm

The broadness delineated by each movement of the baton and left hand should accord with the fervent patriotism of the national anthem. The preparatory movement, as illustrated by the figure, takes the position of the second stroke. The anacrusis of two eighth-notes then sounds forth on the third stroke.

Fig. 62   Ex. **37**.
Siegfried Idyll*   Richard Wagner
Ruhig bewegt (Tranquillo con moto)
Viol. I

Viola   Viol. II

'Cello
* Philharmonia 68.

Calmness, without any apparent exertion on the part of the conductor or the players, should mark this music from the preparatory stroke to the last tone. The left hand plays an important role at the outset when it "lifts" the anacrusis and then sustains the *B* of the First Violins by remaining poised, while the right hand conducts the motive for Viola and 'Cello. Both hands should be used to shape the smooth strokes for this flowing music until the *tranquillo con moto* tempo is well established and under way.

Fig. 63   Ex. **38**. *(See Ex. 3.)*
Prelude from "L'Arlésienne," Suite No. 1   Georges Bizet
Allegro deciso, alla Marcia ♩ = 104
Violin, Viola, 'Cello, Wood-wind & Horn
ff

Just as in the *Minuetto* (Example 34), the anacrusis in this movement is preceded by two quarter-rests constituting preliminary conducting movements. Both of these pulses should be used for preparatory strokes, as indicated by the added dotted lines in the above diagram. These strokes are to be performed in the positions customarily taken by the first and second strokes of the $\frac{4}{4}$ pattern. It cannot be overemphasized that the two opening tones of the "Prelude" must remain unaccented, and that the heavy stroke is reserved to accentuate the first pulse of the first complete bar. It is most essential in this work for the conductor at all times to maintain the correct emphasis on the pulsations.

Fig. 64   **Ex. 39.** *(See Fx. 16.)*

Prelude to "Parsifal"   Richard Wagner

In this case, the quarter-rest at the beginning of the first bar becomes the preparatory stroke. Since the first stroke of the bar is always a down-stroke, this preparatory movement is also performed as a down-stroke. However, it is a comparatively smaller and very much lighter stroke than that which ordinarily marks the first pulsation of the bar. The motive actually begins on the second stroke of the applicable subdivided *sostenuto* diagram.

Fig. 65

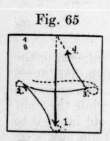

Ex. 40.

Marcia Funebre from Symphony No. 3 ("Eroica")*   Ludwig van Beethoven

*Eulenburg 405.

As the title of this movement indicates, the rhythm should resemble the slow and steady footfalls of a funeral procession commemorating the death of a hero. Whether Beethoven's conception was of a pompous ceremonial march or of more regularly recurring small and even treads cannot, of course, be determined. But the fact remains that there are in each measure four pulses strong enough to warrant a $\frac{4}{8}$ instead of the $\frac{2}{4}$ marking. For this reason, it will be necessary to conduct the third pulsation of the applicable $\frac{4}{8}$ diagram as a preliminary movement before the Strings give sound to the grave and somber motive.

Fig. 66   Ex. 41.

Second Movement
of Symphony in G Minor*   Wolfgang Amadeus Mozart

*Eulenburg 404.

Since the mood is indicated by the *andante* and *piano* markings, only gentle and seemingly effortless baton movements should be made, without losing the distinctness of the six pulses in each bar. The fifth stroke of the $\frac{6}{8}$ figure will become the preliminary motion prior to the anacrusis, which is conducted on the sixth stroke.

For works beginning with one or more rests and a motive which opens on a fractional part of a single metrical pulse, either one complete preceding stroke, or, if necessary, the entire measure should be conducted. It then becomes the primary duty of the left hand to signal the entry with a motion similar to an up-stroke. The same method is used when the anacrusis consists of two or more partial metrical values preceding the first accented pulsation.

The following diagrams and musical examples illustrate the preliminary baton motions for works beginning on one or more subsidiary parts of a single pulsation:

Fig. 67 (See Fig. 56)

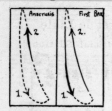

Ex. 42.

Pomp and Circumstance, Military March No. 1*   Edward Elgar, Op. 39
(1857-1934)
Arranged by Adolf Schmid

Allegro con molto fuoco

* Boosey & Co., London. By permission.

Since the composer has specified two preliminary rests, the left hand should
not mark the rhythm.   Only if the rests had been omitted would such signaling
be justified.   In the above example, the baton is immediately set into action at
the first quarter-rest.   The moment the left hand is raised, it brings with it the
fortissimo attack of the full orchestra.   This attack is one of those rare instances
where the anacrusis, instead of the first down-stroke, receives the chief emphasis,
noted by the *marcato* accent.   Actual experience in rehearsing this composition
will show that in order to bring about a united attack of this unusually accentuated phrasing, many attempts will have to be made before the desired result is
attained.

Fig. 68   Ex. **43.**

La Marseillaise
French National Anthem   Credited to Rouget de Lisle
(1768-1836)
Allegro maestoso   French Government's Official Edition

The conductor must, above all, infuse into his orchestra or singers the tremendous upward surge of this high-spirited mood. He must bring about the massed concentration and subordination of every individual energy, until his first vigorous baton stroke releases an arousing and united attack. This stirring national song must be conducted with that impulsive driving strength which made it such an inciting force in the turbulent days of the French Revolution. It would therefore be utterly superfluous and actually detrimental to the entire work to make any deliberating preliminary gestures. The first sixteenth note should follow the baton immediately without any extensive introductory motions whatsoever. During the few seconds in which the conductor gathers his forces, ample preparation will already have been made for the initial attack.

Fig. 69

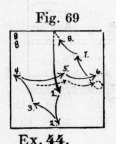

Ex. **44.**
Hungarian Rhapsody No. 1 in F*   Franz Liszt
(1811-1886)
Arranged by Adolf Schmid

Lento quasi Marcia funebre ♩ = 60 quasi 8/8

'Cello & Bass   Horns
Timp.

The anacrusis in this example is in a rhythm very similar to that of the "Marseillaise" (Example 43). However, the moods of the two compositions obviously are strongly contrasted, since Liszt has suggested a slowly winding funeral procession. This *lento* tempo calls for a division into the pulsations of an $\frac{8}{8}$ rhythm. The conducting strokes must be made along smoothly flowing lines and must be free from all jerkiness or unevenness which might disrupt the placidity of the *melos*. This style also applied to the *adagio* $\frac{4}{8}$ rhythm of Beethoven's "Marcia Funebre" (Example 40).

In conclusion, it will be beneficial to review briefly those fundamental precepts that govern preparatory movements of conducting:

(1) In works beginning with a complete measure, the preparatory baton stroke is performed in the position of the last stroke of an appropriate rhythmical diagram. (See Ex. 17-30.)

(2) In works beginning with an anacrusis whose first note is a full metrical pulsation, the preparatory stroke corresponds to the stroke which would precede the first pulse of the anacrusis. (See Ex. 31, 32, 33, 35, 36, 37, 40, 41.)

(3) In works beginning with one or several rests preceding an anacrusis, preparatory strokes mark the rests and the entire measure is conducted. (See Ex. 34, 38, 39.)

(4)   In works beginning with an anacrusis whose first note is a fractional part of a single metrical pulse, the complete stroke, inclusive of the opening subsidiary pulse, should be conducted.   (See Ex. 43, 44.)   In some such instances, the entire measure should be given . (See Ex. 42.)

To each of these precepts it might also be added that the left hand's assistance must be applied with great discretion.   No gesture should ever be idle or superfluous; instead, each motion of the left hand (indicating the dynamics, signaling the entries, establishing the rhythm, *etc.*) must communicate a very definite message.   The adage which advises "let not thy right hand know what thy left hand doeth" certainly does not apply to the art of conducting.   A maximum of cooperation and a sharing of service should control the movements of both hands at all times.

CHAPTER X

HOLDS, RELEASES, AND PAUSES

The clearly delineated interpretation of any musical work demands that no conducting technicality be passed over with undue haste or negligence. The same precision as characterizes the preparatory movements for beginning a composition or phrase, must also mark the *fermata*, the release, and the varied types of pauses, which determine the skilful sustaining and finishing of tones or phrases and produce effective silences.

The most direct approach to these problems probably can best be made by definition and an analytical study of specific musical excerpts.

According to its Italian name, the *fermata* (also termed *corona* and *lunga* in Italian) is defined as a *hold* or a *pause*. The *fermata* marking ⌢ over a note indicates that the time value of the tone is to be lengthened by the conductor according to the composer's musical concept. When the same marking appears over a rest, a bar, or a double bar, a *silent interval* is required; a brief cessation of sound results from a momentary pause of the baton. The purpose of the hold or the pause is to enhance the emotional content or the dramatic suspense of a work. The finishing-off of the tone after a hold or the end of a phrasing may be termed a *release*. (See Plate 12.) At times, a short *breathing pause* (Ger. *Luftpause*) is employed as a very brief silence before the orchestra resumes a motive or takes up a new one. Often the *fermata* is combined with a breathing pause for certain types of phrases; but in other cases, it may also be used effectively alone. The musical examples which follow will serve to clarify the conducting methods to be pursued for the hold, release, and pause.

Ex. 45.

Overture to "A Midsummer Night's Dream"*   Felix Mendelssohn (1809-1847)

*Eulenburg 613.

Fig. 70

Each of the four opening *pianissimo* chords is conducted without any break in the tonal continuity. A release is not made until the end of the fourth *fermata*. An effect is produced very similar to that of these chords if they were to be played on the Piano. The pianist would require no great elevation of the hand in order to move from one to the next. The chords seem to suggest the drawing aside of gossamer curtains revealing to mortal eyes the fanciful revelries at the court of Oberon and Titania. A stray breeze from the heart of the woodlands bears the sound of elfin laughter, merry and mischievous, and of wee feet tripping in sprightly dance. Such a fantasy naturally should dispel every tendency toward harshness or abruptness on the part of either the conductor or the instrumentalists in the performance of this work.

Ex. 46.

Overture to "Ruy Blas" *   Felix Mendelssohn

* Eulenburg 611.

Fig. 71

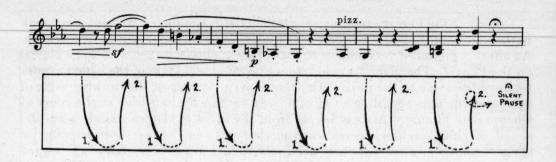

Figure 71, in which each stroke corresponds to the rhythmical and melodic line immediately above it, outlines the right hand conducting-strokes of each measure. Similar strokes are followed out in a reversed direction by the left hand. The *fermata* in the fourth measure is released by an emphatic outward gesture, following which the baton conducts the preparatory stroke introducing the next *alla breve* motive in an *allegro molto* tempo. This motive then proceeds to the last note in this excerpt, after which a silent pause occurs.

Ex. 47.

First Movement of Symphony No. 5 (in C Minor)* Ludwig van Beethoven

*Eulenburg 402.

Fig. 72

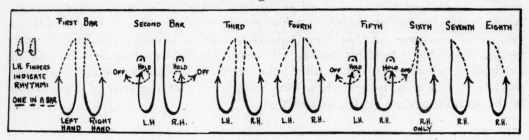

Fig. 73

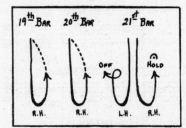

The opening motive, the "knocks of Fate" (See page 7), calls for a steady *fermata*, held by both hands. Any *diminuendo* weakens the dramatic concept. The *fermata* is followed by a short silence, which gives the impression of listening for the second "knock". It is important, after the second *fermata* has been released, to make a breathing pause; otherwise the *fortissimo* effect smothers the *piano* passage of the Second Violins. This "breath" should not be exaggerated into a General Pause. From the 6th measure on, the motive is continued *piano* and develops into *forte*. The last three chords are short—except the First Violin's sustained high *G*. (See Figure 73.) The conductor signals the release with the left hand and at the same time "holds" the Violin's *G* with the right. After the release, a preparatory movement again introduces the Fate Motive. This scheme of conducting applies to much of the First Movement.

Ex. 48.

First Movement of Symphony No. 5 (in C Minor)*   Ludwig van Beethoven

* Eulenburg 402.

This example presents two silent measures which are to be conducted with small and unostentatious one-in-a-bar motions. Any broad or powerful gestures would, naturally, be out of place. A distinct rhythmical value is inherent in these two silent measures, so that their pulsations can be sensed, even though they remain inaudible. For this reason, the baton should never come to a halt in conducting silent bars. In reality, the rhythmical and melodic lines have reached no full stop; instead these bars seem to be marking time in expectation of the opening motive, which follows them.

Ex. 49.

Third Movement of Symphony No. 5 (in C Minor)*   Ludwig van Beethoven

*Eulenburg 402.

After the *fermata* at the 8th bar, the marking //, indicating a short breathing pause, has been made by the composer. This pause acts as a safeguard to assure a precise re-entry of the *Scherzo* motive's anacrusis. After the *fermata* in the 18th bar has been released, a slight breathing pause will be very necessary, even though it has not been marked in the score. This minute pause is absolutely essential to the effectiveness of the *fortissimo* Horn passage which follows at once. The release of the second *fermata* is best signaled by the left hand while the right hand conducts the brief preparatory motion for the Horn motive. If this particular release were to be conducted by the right hand, a false sense of finality would be conveyed to both the orchestra and the listeners. For the sake of continuity, it is, therefore, more practical to employ the left hand for the release. Just as in the telling of a story, each sentence is oriented toward the highest point of interest and then towards the final unraveling of the plot, so musical phrases must also be deftly turned from the beginning of a composition to the last tone. Never should the slightest technical awkwardness be permitted to disrupt the continuity and, as a result, to mar the enjoyment of the listeners. The only ideal to uphold in musical performances is absolute perfection.

Ex. 50
Overture to "Die Zauberflöte"
   (The Magic Flute)*
                                            Wolfgang Amadeus Mozart

*Eulenburg 614

Fig. 74

17606

The *adagio* has been marked *alla breve* and should be conducted according to a subdivided *alla breve* diagram. (It could also have been marked $\frac{4}{4}$; see page 35.) It is advantageous to make an additional subdivision of the last half of the second stroke in conducting the first, second, and third measures. This extra pulse is necessary in order to gain a precise attack after the pauses. The release of the first chord is signalled by a small, quick gesture, after which the baton remains in position for the briefest of intervals before it moves upward almost unobserved, and gains an added impetus for the anacrusis. After the anacrusis of the melody, which begins in the third measure, the right hand alone will be necessary to guide the smooth *legato* melodic line of the First Violins, accompanied by Second Violins and Violas, and the secondary theme for 'Cellos and Basses.

Ex. **51**.

First Movement of Symphony in D Minor*   César Franck

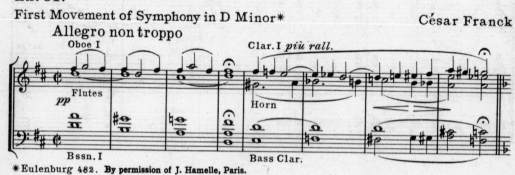

*Eulenburg 482. **By permission of J. Hamelle, Paris.**

Fig. 75

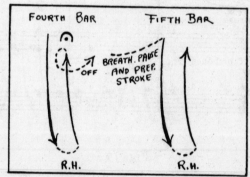

After the *fermata* of the 4th bar has been released, a breathing pause must be produced. The reason for this natural pause is derived from the change in tone-color after the *fermata*. In the first four bars of this excerpt, the instrumentation calls for the Oboe accompanied by two Flutes and Bassoon. Immediately after the released pause, a preparatory stroke leads to the continuation of the motive for First Clarinet accompanied by Horns, and Bass Clarinet. This change of instruments and the brief interval during which this preparatory stroke is being made suffice as a breathing pause or *Luftpause*. The actual marking of the breathing pause has been deliberately omitted from the score in order to avoid the risk of "cutting" the even continuity of the work into a series of short, disjointed melodic fragments. It is important for this *pianissimo* movement to maintain a gentle smoothness in the conducting strokes, for which the use of the right hand alone will be most appropriate.

Ex. 52.

First Movement of Symphony in D Minor *   César Franck

Allegro non troppo

*Eulenburg 482. **By permission of J. Hamelle, Paris.**

Fig. 76

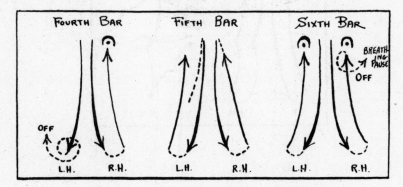

This excerpt is almost similar to the preceding example. After the first four bars, a change of instrumentation is effected. However, in this case, the *fermata* on the sustained F♯ for Oboe acts as a kind of bridge extended over the release of the harmony and leading directly into the phrase for Flute, Clarinet, and English Horn. For the second and third *fermate*, the releases are made with very little exertion. The subsequent preparatory strokes will, as in Example 51, automatically produce brief breathing pauses and will bring about the most natural phraseology.

Ex. 53.

First Movement of Symphony in D Minor *   César Franck

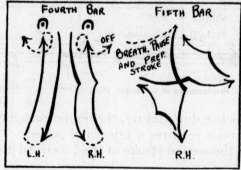

*Eulenburg 482. By permission of J. Hamelle, Paris.

Fig. 77

This excerpt is made up of the Second Subject, played by Flutes and Oboes, with a subsidiary phrase for 'Cellos combined with the other Wood-winds. In the 4th measure, it will be advantageous to guide the 'Cello motive with the baton, while the left hand holds and releases the harmony. The natural result following the releases will be a breathing-pause which occurs simultaneously with the preparatory stroke before the re-entry of the *Lento*. Even though it has not been marked in the score, this breathing pause is necessary in practice, in order to prevent a blurred entry of the motive. The left hand, which is in position to anticipate cues, tempers the effectiveness of the *forte*-to-*piano* nuances.

Ex. 54.

Second Movement of Symphony in D Minor* César Franck

*Eulenburg 482, page 80. By permission of J. Hamelle, Paris.

This passage depicts a dual nature; the tempo changes with the moods. The transition between moods requires a breathing pause. The preparatory stroke takes the direction of the second stroke of the $\frac{3}{4}$ metrical diagram; the third stroke begins the anacrusis.

Ex. 55.

First Movement of Symphony No. 5 (in C Minor)* Ludwig van Beethoven

*Eulenburg 402.

A climactic point in the struggle against Fate, this passage seems to transform the Oboe into the human voice.   The conqueror pauses for a moment and reflects on the ephemeral nature of all things, but remains unswerving and undefeated. This *cadenza* will require no conducting motions.   After the three chords and the *fermata*, sustained by the Oboe, a nod from the conductor will suffice to give the cue to the Oboe soloist who continues freely.   Any variations of opinion as to the interpretation of this *cadenza* should, of course, have already been satisfactorily reconciled at the rehearsals before the public performance.   During the playing of the *cadenza*, the conductor naturally remains in a position ready to give the preparatory movement which precedes the return of the Fate Motive.

Ex. 56.

Scheherazade*   Nikolai Rimsky-Korsakoff

*Eulenburg 493. With permission of M. P. Belaieff, Leipzig.

The General Pause, or the *Grande Pause*, as it is also termed, is indicated by the initials *G.P.* or the sign of the *fermata* placed above one or more complete, silent measures.   During a Grand Pause, like those in the 5th and 7th measures of the above excerpt, the entire orchestra remains silent.   After the last note of the 4th measure has been released, the most practical manner in which to conduct the silent measure is with a simple down-stroke, instead of following out a metrical diagram.   The usual up-stroke then leads to the next bar.

A careful analytical study of the foregoing musical examples (Ex. 45-56) and diagrams resolves itself into the following salient points regarding the conducting of holds, releases, and pauses:

(1)   The *fermata* over a note or a rest lengthens the normal time value. For the duration of the *fermata*, the baton comes to a temporary halt.   (See Ex. 45, 46, 47, 49, 50, 51, 52, 53, 54, 55, 56.)

(2)   The release is indicated by the baton or the left hand which figuratively casts off the tone which has been prolonged by the *fermata*.   Usually the left hand releases the hold, while a preparatory stroke of the baton leads to the next tone.   (See above examples for *fermata*.)

(3) Certain passages containing two or more interwoven thematic subjects require a double conducting action carried out simultaneously by the baton and the left hand. (See Ex. 53.)

(4) The breathing pause or *Luftpause* calls for a very short cessation of sound. This is caused by a quick release, after which the baton pauses for the briefest of intervals before it proceeds into the preparatory stroke. The breathing pause may also occur simultaneously with the preparatory stroke. (See Ex. 49.)

(5) The breathing pause frequently occurs between radical or subtle changes in musical moods, instrumental coloring, tempos, or dynamics. When the marking of a necessary breathing pause has been omitted from the score, the conductor's musicianship must guide him in supplying it. (See Ex. 47, 49, 51, 52, 53, 54.)

(6) Silent measures require small, unostentatious conducting gestures. Since the rhythmic and melodic line continues to make itself felt during silent measures, the baton is never permitted to come to a standstill. (See Ex. 48.)

(7) The cadenza is freely performed by the soloist and therefore requires no baton motions. The conductor remains in readiness to give the preparatory stroke at the conclusion of the cadenza. (See Ex. 55.)

(8) The General Pause (G.P) indicates one or more silent measures for the entire orchestra. One down-stroke of the baton suffices for each measure of the General Pause. (See Ex. 56.)

CHAPTER XI

THE END-STROKE

One of the most essential factors of a skilful conducting technique is the absolute mastery of the end-stroke. An effective conclusion of a musical work can be obtained only when the end-stroke produces a decisive and unambiguous sense of finality. (*See Plate 13.*)

A careful distinction must be drawn between the end-stroke that concludes the first or an intermediate movement of a symphony, and the stroke that closes the *finale*. The same distinction exists for the sections of a suite or a series of dramatic excerpts. A unity of conception must prevail from the first page of the score to the last. For this reason, the end-stroke that concludes a section or a movement should have a certain degree of finality, and, at the same time, should suggest both a suspended atmosphere and a further development in the next part.

After the release of the last tone of a section, one or both hands must come back to position instantaneously and remain in readiness for the next movement. The natural result of this procedure is that the atmosphere still remains musically charged in the silent transition between movements, so that the inherent unity of the work is kept intact. On the other hand, a most disrupting "short circuit" would be incurred if the conductor deemed it necessary to drop his hands completely after each movement, and then, perhaps, to search for a misplaced handkerchief to mop his musical brow before he continued with the work. However, by keeping his hands in position, the conductor also forestalls the possibility that premature applause of the audience may raucously break the unity of the musical conception.

The manner in which the concluding strokes are performed is dictated largely by the mood of the composition and the extent to which the conductor feels this mood. A vigorously energetic close and a gently quiescent one naturally motivate contrasted types of end-strokes. A variety of cases is presented in the following musical excerpts:

Ex. **57.**

First Movement of Symphony No. 3 ("Eroica")* Ludwig van Beethoven
Allegro con brio

*Eulenburg 405.

58

The stirring *crescendo* leading to a *fortissimo* close of this *allegro con brio* movement demands an impetuously forceful down-stroke for each of the last three chords.   Immediately after the last chord, the left hand returns to position and directs attention toward the next movement.   In this way, concentrated interest heightens the dramatic contrast of the opening *piano* motive in the "Marcia Funebre".   (See Ex. 40.)

Ex. 58
Marcia Funebre and Scherzo
  of Symphony No. 3 ("Eroica")*   Ludwig van Beethoven

*Eulenburg 405.

Fig. 78

For the ending of the funeral procession, the mourners' last expression of grief rises in the *sforzato* chord and is resolved in a final noble resignation to the passing of the hero.   The subdued atmosphere is sufficiently sustained by the *fermata*, so that immediately after its release, two quick finger-signals indicating a one-in-a-bar rhythm will be the only prerequisites for the entry of the *pianissimo Scherzo*.

Ex. 59.

Scherzo and Finale of Symphony No. 3("Eroica")*   Ludwig van Beethoven

*Eulenburg 405.

The three *fortissimo* chords of the *Scherzo* are treated in an impulsive manner very similar to that concluding the First Movement. (See Ex. 57.) It will be observed in the above example that Beethoven wrote a *fermata* on a silent measure following the chords. This precautionary device keeps up the attention and the vigor necessary to the first *fortissimo* theme of the *Finale allegro molto*. The silent measure is conducted with a single down-stroke which returns to position and prolongs the rest, thereby preventing a disjointed transition from one unit to another of a single conception.

Ex. 60.

Finale of Symphony No. 3("Eroica")*   Ludwig van Beethoven

*Eulenburg 405.

The three decisive chords, which conclude the entire symphony, must be finished off most emphatically. They should be conducted so forcefully as to leave not the slightest doubt as to their absolute finality. The *fermata* over the rest may be disregarded, since the baton and left hand do not return to position, but have already completed their work after the last down-stroke. In a sense, this *fermata* represents that momentary breathless pause between the end of an intensely gripping drama and the final burst of applause. The *fermata* over a rest in the last bar was the traditional marking simply denoting the end in the works of the older masters; it rarely occurs in present-day usage.

The fact is self-evident that the end-strokes discussed for the excerpts from Beethoven's "Eroica" Symphony (Ex. 57, 58, 59, 60) serve as models applicable to almost any other style of composition. Whether it is a light gavotte or an animated concert overture, the intrinsic nature and the dynamics of a composition are the factors which re-shape the fundamentals into those individual strokes best adapted to the work in question. There must be no incompatibility or clash of temperaments between the end-stroke and the mood of the music which is interpreted. An appropriate kind of end-stroke often can bring the most insignificant piece of music to a successful and satisfying conclusion. On the other hand, an inept end-stroke can kill a masterwork and reduce the acme of musical art to ineffective tonal triviality.

Each of the following supplementary musical examples presents an individual type of conclusion and end-stroke:

Ex. 61.

Second Movement of the "Unfinished" Symphony*   Franz Schubert

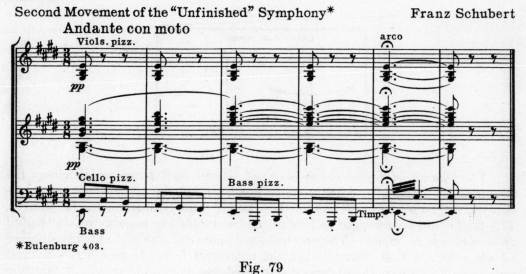

*Eulenburg 403.

Fig. 79

The end-stroke must express the quietude of this *pianissimo* conclusion. No excessive effort should be made in releasing the *fermata*. Instead, each tone should be allowed to die out gradually until the gentle release of the final pause, like a quiet nod, indicates the end.

Ex. 62.
Overture to "Oberon" *   Carl Maria von Weber

*Eulenburg 607.

Fig. 80

The summit of joyfulness is attained in the final pæan which closes the Overture to "Oberon". After a single down-stroke, the last tremendous wave of joy is intensified by the *fermata*, whose power must be sustained unflinchingly. This final chord is prolonged as long as the conductor can possibly retain the full flood of tone in his grasp. The psychological moment in which to make a decisive release comes at that instant when the conductor feels the orchestra's natural endurance limitations threatening to diminish the volume of tone. It may too frequently be observed that in performing this type of *fermata* and end-stroke, certain conductors commit an unpardonable breach of good taste. Such practices as quivering with uncontrolled excitement or frantically shaking the fists to exhort the players to greater strength of tone can only be condemned. Observation of such frenzied conclusion will usually reveal an actual decrease in the response, since the orchestra members justifiably resent the conductor's pseudo-"showmanship" and over-exuberance. It is wise to remember that a display of antics bordering on the pathological is not necessary to the performance of overwhelmingly jubilant music.

Ex. 63.

Overture, "The Roman Carnival" *   Hector Berlioz

Allegro vivace ♩. = 156

[musical score]

*Eulenburg 620.

Fig. 81

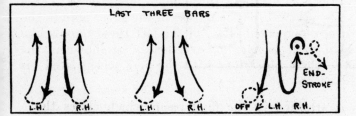

(NOTE: The rapidity of the tempo, as evidenced by the marking (♩. = 156), necessitates an economy of movement. For only two strong pulses in each bar, the use of a duple conducting scheme is most imperative. See Ex. 63 and 22.)

Comparison shows that the method of performing the end-stroke in this excerpt is unlike that of Example 62 because of the instrumentation in the last measure, which demands separate tonal releases. As indicated by Figure 81, in the last bar the entire String Choir and Percussion are silenced by the left hand, while the baton sustains the scintilating metallic timbre produced by the Brass and Wood-wind. There is no *diminuendo* whatsoever, and the final release is taken off with an abrupt downward force. It will be noted that the extra curve in the end-stroke is a visual device which gains the attention of every player and effects a simultaneous tonal release.

Ex. 64
"Carillon" from "L'Arlésienne," Suite No. 1*

Georges Bizet

Allegretto moderato ♩. = 104

*Eulenburg 828.

Fig. 82

A strict one-in-a-bar rhythm is adhered to throughout this excerpt. (See Example 18.) The end-stroke is reserved for the release of the short note in the final measure. The actual aurally perceived effect of the last three bars is like a single chord combination held by a *fermata*. Nevertheless, as shown in the diagram, the rhythmical figure—three pulsations with the first accentuated—is indicated by the strokes of the baton.

Ex. 65
Carnival Overture*

Anton Dvořák
(1841-1904)

Allegro ♩ = 132

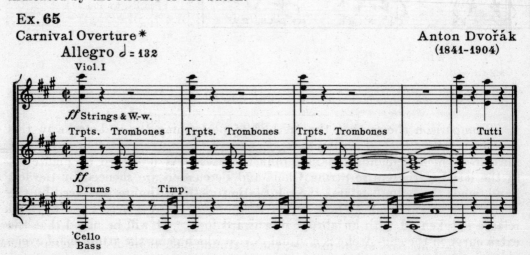

*With special permission of the original publisher, N. Simrock, Musikverlag, Leipzig. Other important overtures by Dvořák, which are published by N. Simrock, are "My Home", Op. 62; "Husitzka", Op. 67; "In the Nature", Op. 91; and "Otello", Op. 93.

Fig. 83

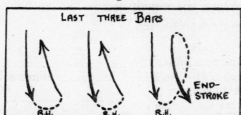

The dominant feature of the *coda* of this Overture is produced by the *fortissimo* call of the Trombone Choir reinforced by the Timpani. The remaining orchestral forces, including the Percussion instruments, are called into action to emphasize the first chord in each bar. The Trombone call is extended into a *crescendo* founded on a roll in the Timpani. This *crescendo* is finished off by two final short chords. As a safeguard against any weakening anticlimactic effect, the main stress should be on the second of these two chords, an emphatic end-stroke.

Ex. 66.

Overture to "Die Fledermaus"*   Johann Strauss
(1825–1899)

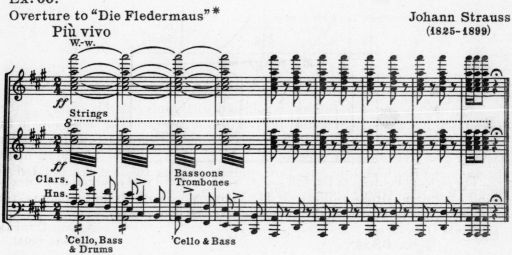

*Edition Cranz 2103.

Fig. 84

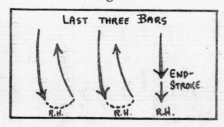

In the four bars of the motive, the rhythmic pulsations of this excerpt must be most markedly felt according to the indicated dynamic stresses. In the concluding bar, the first sixteenth note is a sharp and forceful down-stroke, carrying the full weight of the conclusion. The actual end-stroke then, with lightning rapidity, re-echoes this decisive stroke.

Ex. 67.
"Rosen aus dem Süden"*
(Roses from the South)   Johann Strauss
Waltz

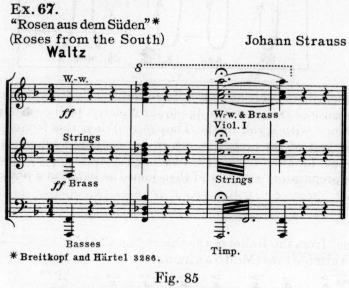

* Breitkopf and Härtel 3286.

Fig. 85

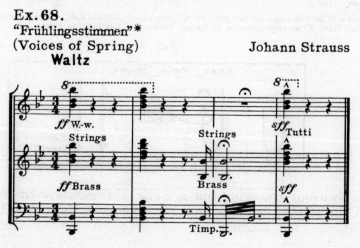

The *fermata* holds over the full orchestral tone until it is easily and spiritedly cut off by the end-stroke as illustrated in Figure 85. Both the left hand and the baton carry out similar motions for conducting the final release.

Ex. 68.
"Frühlingsstimmen"*
(Voices of Spring)   Johann Strauss
Waltz

* Breitkopf and Härtel 3287.

Fig. 86

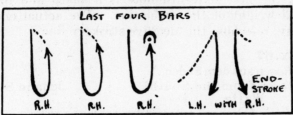

The conclusion of this excerpt differs significantly from that of the preceding example because of the drop into the lower registers of the sustained Strings and Brass combined with a roll in the Timpani. When this *fermata* is about to be released, the rest of the orchestra, which has remained temporarily silent, must be in readiness for the final *sf tutti* finish. To serve this purpose, the left hand rises as in a preparatory stroke and then joins the baton in a powerful descending end-stroke.

Ex. 69.

"Catalane" from the Ballet of the Opera "Le Cid" *   Jules Massenet
(1842-1912)

Très animé ♩= 108 (Molto animato)

* Published with the following authorizations: For the countries of Germany and the former Austro-Hungarian monarchy, by Adolf Fürstner, Berlin W; for other countries, by Heugel, Éditeur, 2bis Rue Vivienne, Paris.

Fig. 87

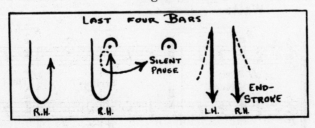

This vivacious dance, in a one-in-a-bar rhythm, has an unusual and effective close. A rapidly twirling sensation is produced by the trill in the Wood-winds and Strings.   The flurry of sound is suddenly arrested by a silent pause, followed an instant later by a crashing finish for the entire orchestra.   The left hand comes to the assistance of the baton only for the forcible end-stroke.

Ex. 70.

"Madrilène" from the Ballet of the Opera "Le Cid"*   Jules Massenet

* Published with the following authorizations: For the countries of Germany and the former Austro-Hungarian monarchy, by Adolf Fürstner, Berlin W; for other countries, by Heugel, Éditeur, 2bis Rue Vivienne, Paris.

Fig. 88

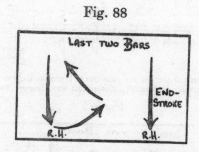

The pulsations in this dance are based on one rhythmical figure without wide deviation and without any elaboration for the *coda*.   The evenness of the rhythm grows heavier and more marked in the next to the last bar and halts with an accentuated stamp.   For this reason, the end-stroke requires decidedly more vigor than the strokes in the preceding measures.

Ex. 71.
March from "Scènes Pittoresques"*

Jules Massenet

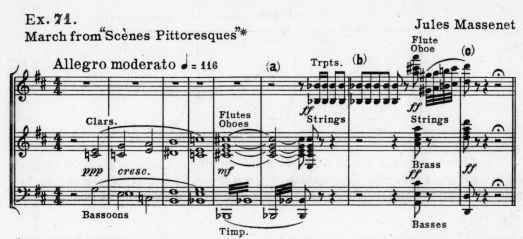

* Published with the following authorizations: For the countries of Germany and the former Austro-Hungarian monarchy, by B. Schott's Söhne, Mainz; for the British Empire, by Joseph Williams, Ltd., London, owners of the copyright; for other countries, by Heugel, Éditeur, 2bis Rue Vivienne, Paris.

Fig. 89

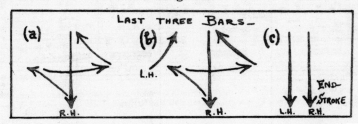

The conviviality that would be present at a rustic church festival is represented in this march. Sounding like the distant tones of an organ postlude, the Clarinets and Bassoons are augmented by the Horns, Flutes, Oboes, and Strings, with a deep roll in the Timpani. A Trumpet-call then announces the end of the festivities and points to the unique *coda*. The action of the left hand reinforces the baton strokes for the last two *fortissimo* chords.

Ex. 72.
Introduction and Mazurka from the Ballet "La Source"*

Léo Delibes
(1836-1891)

Tempo di Mazurka

* Published with the following authorizations: For Italy, by G. Ricordi & Company, Milan; for other countries, by Heugel, Éditeur, 2bis Rue Vivienne, Paris.

Fig. 90

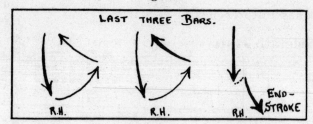

In this excerpt, the baton and left hand should lay particular stress on the *tutti fortissimo* of the final three chords.   Since the end falls on the second stroke of the bar, a strong and weighted down-stroke must be used, as shown in Figure 90.

Ex. 73.

Angelus from "Scènes Pittoresques"*   Jules Massenet

Andante sostenuto ♩ = 56

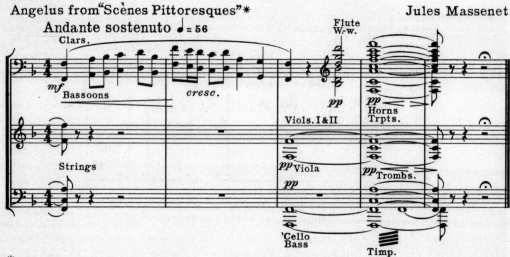

* Published with the following authorizations: For the countries of Germany and the former Austro-Hungarian monarchy, by B. Schott's Söhne, Mainz; for the British Empire, by Joseph Williams, Ltd., London, owners of the copyright; for other countries, by Heugel, Éditeur, 2bis Rue Vivienne. Paris.

Fig. 91 ·

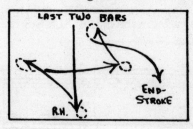

As the title suggests, "The Angelus" closes in a mood of utmost tranquillity. In the second pulsation of the next to the last bar, a momentary surge is felt in the *pp crescendo* for entire orchestra, including Timpani. Immediately on the third and fourth pulsations, the prolonged tones are gently diminished until they are finally hushed by a relaxed and easy drop of the baton.

Plate 8—PIANISSIMO ATTACK

Plate 9—FORTISSIMO ATTACK

Plate 10—CUE FOR ENTRY

Plate 11—DELICATE PHRASING

Plate 12— **RELEASE OF FERMATA (HOLD)**

Plate 13—END-STROKE

Thus, the manner in which the end-stroke is made naturally varies according to the dynamics of each individual composition. Each type of end-stroke must bring to both the hearers and the performers a satisfying feeling of relieved tension after the suspense of an emotionally stimulating work. When an end-stroke fails to convey the effect of a conclusion, the audience is left in an uneasy state of suddenly deflated anticipation. It is as though the orchestra's rising toward a grand climax were a sky-rocket which had failed to burst into a glorious rain of stars, but had simply sputtered feebly, then dropped to earth again.

In conclusion, the following generalizations regarding the end-stroke might be reiterated:

(1) Whether the end-stroke is directed downward or sidewise, it must convey a definite sense of finality in order to be effective. (See Ex. 64, 69.)

(2) If another movement or section of a composition is to follow, unity and an atmosphere of suspense must be maintained. Neither the orchestra nor the audience will experience a "let-down" between the parts of a work if one or both hands return to conducting position. (See Ex. 57, 58, 59.)

(3) The manner of performing the end-stroke is greatly dependent upon individual problems of instrumentation, dynamics, and rhythm. It is not unusual, therefore, to find cases which may require two down-strokes in the final bar. (See Ex. 65, 66, 72.)

(4) The character of the end-stroke is derived almost solely from the mood of the composition. Music of a quiet, calm nature needs a corresponding type of stroke (See Ex. 61); in marked contrast, a forceful end-stroke is required for an exultant, triumphant finish. (See Ex. 63, 65.)

CHAPTER XII

CADENZAS

The cadenza, an ingeniously wrought thematic ornamentation, is characterized by spontaneity and freedom of the imagination. Whether it is a simple embellishment of a single chord or an elaborate maze of flourishes, the well-performed cadenza gives the impression of freely developed and highly skilled extemporaneous improvising.

In the past, the cadenza provided an opportunity for singers or instrumentalists to display their versatility and mastery of technique. The soloist seized a pause or a *fermata* as the starting point for the impromptu invention of the most intricate musical figuration. It was probably the abuse of this liberty which induced later composers, from Beethoven on, to write out cadenzas in complete detail. Among present-day soloists, a reversion to the older freedom may be noted in individual paraphrases on the cadenza as set down by the composer.

Because of the cadenza's seeming release from any confining musical form, the conductor must take great care to study the soloist's particular interpretation. Only after such analysis and actual memorization is the conductor equipped to join the cadenza to the orchestral entries without any audible crudity.

During the solo performance of the cadenza, both the conductor and orchestra become listeners for the moment. All conducting movements cease and the complete range of interpretation is left to the soloist. However, as the soloist is completing the trill, which is the conventional sign of the close of the cadenza, the conductor quietly raises his baton in readiness for the orchestra's taking over the work and carrying it forward to further development or to the conclusion.

The musical examples in this chapter (Ex. 74-86) present a variety of types and uses of the cadenza. Besides its purely ornamental purposes, the cadenza may serve as a bridge between two motives, moods, movements, melodies, or keys. In large symphonic works and in concertos, the cadenza frequently is the means of linking all of the major themes and rounding out the work in a brilliant *coda*.

Examples of the cadenza follow:

Ex. 74.

Overture to "Raymond"*

Ambroise Thomas
(1811-1896)

* Published with the authorization of Heugel, Éditeur, 2bis Rue Vivienne, Paris.

Fig. 92

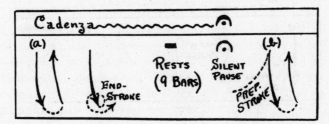

After the first sustained *A* of the solo 'Cello, the rest of the Strings and the Wood-wind recede into silence. Conducting motions are temporarily halted, and the cadenza is freely executed by the soloist. At the end of the cadenza, sufficient time allowance is made for the *fermata* over the pause. During this silent pause, the conductor raises his baton for the preparatory stroke which will lead the orchestra into the next bar.

Ex. 75.
Overture to "Orphée aux Enfers"*   J. Offenbach
                                                        (1819-1880)
Allegro vivace

*B. Schott and Sons, Mainz.

Fig. 93

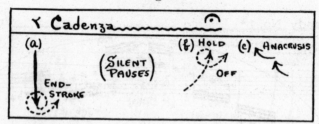

After the strong down-stroke which releases the *tutti sforzato,* a glance or a nod from the conductor acts as an indication to the Violin soloist to play the cadenza *ad libitum.*   On the *fermata* over the final half-note of the cadenza, the conductor again raises the baton to sustain and release the tone.   As shown in Figure 93, no additional preparatory stroke is needed, since the released *fermata* suffices for the accurate entry of the *allegretto* anacrusis.

Ex. 76.

Hungarian Rhapsody No. 1*   Franz Liszt

*N. Simrock, Berlin-Leipzig.

Fig. 94

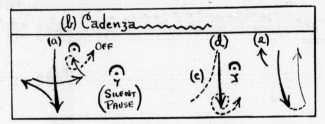

During the trill, the orchestra's *fermata* is released by the left hand. The baton remains stationary during the silent pause. In order to unite the orchestra with the last tone of the cadenza, the preparatory stroke is conducted simultaneously with the last sixteenth-note of the candenza.

Ex. 77.
Hungarian Rhapsody No. 1*   Franz Liszt

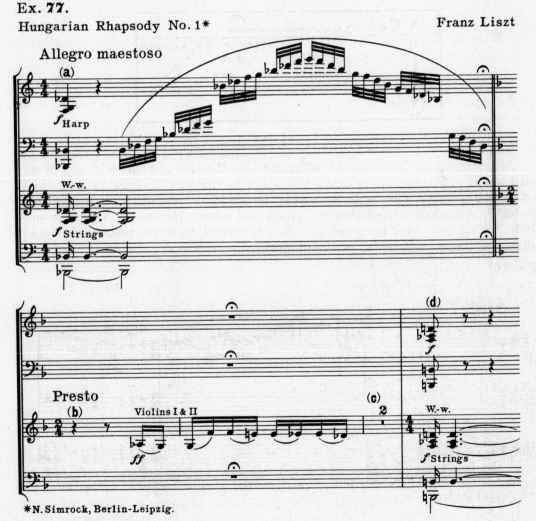

*N. Simrock, Berlin-Leipzig.

Fig. 95

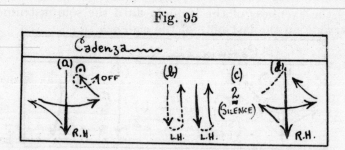

This Harp cadenza is built on a single arpeggio. The conductor sustains the Strings and Wood-wind during the entire arpeggio, until both the orchestra and solo finish simultaneously. Within the prolonged silent pause which follows, a novelty in the form of a miniature *presto* phrase is introduced. It is advisable in this case to guide the Violins with the left hand only. If the conductor prefers not to use the left hand, he might unobtrusively indicate the tempo with the baton. In either case, the conductor must be ready for the attack of the next tone by Wood-wind, Strings, and Harp.

Ex. 78.
Scheherazade*

Nikolai Rimsky-Korsakoff

*Eulenburg 493. With permission of M. P. Belaieff, Leipzig.

Fig. 96

In this example, the cadenza is performed by the Second Trombone and First Trumpet, while the baton sustains the steady tremolo of the First and Second Violins. For the first pulsation of the tremolo, a subdivided downstroke should be used. The baton then continues on its smooth upward course and prolongs the evenness of the tremolo until the solo instruments have completed the *fermata* on the last note of the cadenza.

Ex. 79.

Scheherazade*   Nikolai Rimsky-Korsakoff

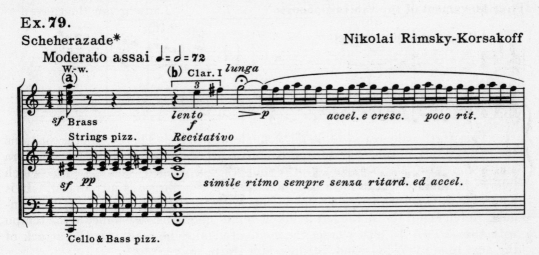

*Eulenburg 493. With permission of M. P. Belaieff, Leipzig.

Fig. 97

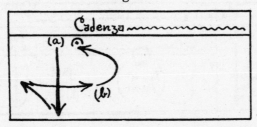

The conductor must make sure of absolute adherence to the rhythm and tempo for the opening *pizzicato* pulsations of each bar. On the *fermata*, the baton pauses. At a sign from the conductor, the solo Clarinet proceeds at will, while the accompanying Strings continue to reiterate the chord evenly, irrespective of any *tempo rubato* deviations in the cadenza. The same procedure is repeated for the second bar.

Ex. 80.

First Movement of the Violin Concerto*

Ludwig van Beethoven

*Eulenburg 701.

Fig. 98

The last three bars lead directly to the cadenza. The soloist then is entirely free to execute the passage-work in any manner he chooses. (The cadenza in the excerpt is based on one by Lauterbach.) The final trill is the formal cue for the conductor's up-stroke in anticipation of the next measure.

Ex. 81.

Third Movement of the Violin Concerto* Ludwig van Beethoven

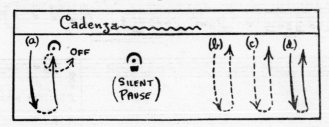

*Eulenburg 701.

Fig. 99

This example is in many respects similar to the preceding excerpt. (See Ex. 80.) The *fermata* on the *A* begins the cadenza which eventually leads into a concluding trill. (This cadenza, as given, is also adapted from Lauterbach.) In this case, the conductor resumes actual conducting motions, two strokes in a bar, one complete measure before the anacrusis.

Ex. 82.

Excerpt from the Violin Concerto* Felix Mendelssohn

Allegro molto appassionato

*Eulenburg 702.

Fig. 100

This cadenza grows out of an arpeggio based on the orchestral development. At the release of the *tutti sf*, the solo violinist continues the arpeggio passages. The actual conducting is resumed one full measure before the entry of the Flute, Oboe, and First Violin.

Ex. 83.

Piano Concerto No. 5 (The "Emperor")*   Ludwig van Beethoven

*Eulenburg 706.

Fig. 101

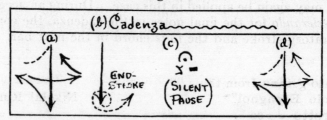

This excerpt is begun with strong and strictly rhythmic strokes of an adapted $\frac{4}{4}$ pattern, enabling the Piano soloist to make a decisive entry for the cadenza. The *espressivo* passage will be performed with a slight *ritardando* or *ritenuto*, which serves as the conductor's cue for the next preparatory stroke, which will join the cadenza to the orchestra in a *fortissimo* chord.

Ex. 84.

Piano Concerto No. 5 (The "Emperor")*   Ludwig van Beethoven

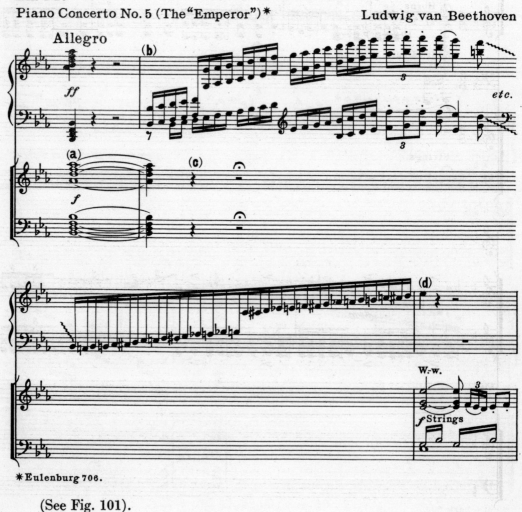

*Eulenburg 706.

(See Fig. 101).

Precisely the same principles as those discussed for the foregoing cadenza (Example 83) may again be applied in this case. During an accentuated *ritenuto* or a slight *accelerando* for the final notes in the cadenza, the conductor is ready for the preparatory stroke and the *forte* chord in the next bar.

Ex. 85.

Scena e canto gitano from the
  "Capriccio Espagnol"*   Nikolai Rimsky-Korsakoff
  Allegretto ♩.= 69

*Eulenburg 842. With permission of M. P. Belaieff, Leipzig.

Fig. 102

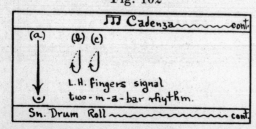

(NOTE: the tempo marking, ♩. = 69, calls for duple rhythm, as in Ex. 63. The first down-stroke (a) is to be considered a single unit in itself. The finger signals (b and c) represent two pulsations of one bar. The three sixteenth-notes which begin the cadenza are a part of the second of these pulsations.)

A firm down-stroke of the baton vigorously attacks the Snare Drum roll, as illustrated by Figure 102. Two small rhythmic pulses, marked by one or two fingers of the left hand, indicate the tempo and act as cues for beginning the Brass cadenza. The interpretation of this cadenza should have been so thoroughly rehearsed previous to public performance that the six players can execute this section practically without actual conducting, even though the controlling force of the conductor still makes itself felt. At the height of the brilliant Brass flare, a slight finger-signal suffices to produce a quick *diminuendo* and release. The roll of the Snare Drum then continues as a *ppp* accompaniment for the cadenza of the solo Violin.

Ex. 86.

Scena and Aria, No. 14, from
"Lucia di Lammermoor"*

Gaetano Donizetti
(1797-1848)

Allegro

li - ce!
morn - ing!

Oh gio-ja__ che si - sen - te,   oh gio-ja
Oh joy un-told, un-fath-om'd,   With-in my

*G. Schirmer, Inc., Vocal Score, page 194.

Fig. 103

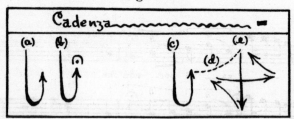

The conducting of works containing vocal cadenzas does not differ essentially from those with instrumental cadenzas. This excerpt from "Lucia" is begun with the regular *arioso* conducting strokes according to a ⁴⁄₄ form. For the silent pauses (See a, b, c), a single down-stroke at the beginning of each bar is made. On the first syllable of the word *felice*, preparation is made for the down-stroke which falls on the second syllable, the cue for the *tutti* orchestral entry.

Ex. 87.

Excerpt from the Duet of
Norma and Adalgisa in "Norma"*

Vincenzo Bellini
(1801-1834)

Andante

Norma

Più lu - sin - ghe,__ ah più spe-ran-za pres - so a mor-te il__cor__ non

Adalgisa

Ah pie-ta - de __ di lor ti toc-chi, se__ non hai di te__ pie-

Andante

p Strings   *sempre staccato*

*G. Ricordi & Co., Milan, Vocal Score, pages 178-179.

Fig. 104

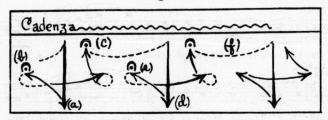

The conducting of this cadenza for two solo voices observes, as in the previous example, the principles applicable to instrumental cadenzas. However, in this specific case, conducting motions are indispensable in order to gain precise entries of the short chords accompanying the cadenza. A down-stroke at (a) brings in the chord of the first bar of the cadenza. The stroke then moves to the left and pauses as long as the singers hold the *fermata* at (*b*). A brief preparatory movement follows each hold and leads to the next pulsation. Immediately after the *pianissimo* chord is brought in by the third stroke, the baton continues its motion and then pauses at (*c*) until the singers simultaneously reach the syllables *spe-* and *non*. A slight preparatory stroke then leads to the down-stroke (*d*) for the first chord of the next bar. After the pause at (*e*) followed by two chords and another pause, the conductor's preparatory stroke (*f*) anticipates the conclusion of the cadenza.

It is advisable for the conductor and the soloists to rehearse the duet with the Piano apart from the orchestra in order to solve any differences of opinion in interpretative problems. The duet should then be performed without any technical impediment at the rehearsal with the orchestra.

Each of the foregoing examples (Ex. 74-87) has shown that the dominant feature of the cadenza is its apparent abandonment and freedom. The soloist is at liberty to work out the cadenza figuration independently, while the conductor mentally follows and gives the cue for the orchestra to resume the work. It, therefore, becomes the obvious responsibility of both conductor and soloist during rehearsals to meet on a cooperative basis regarding interpretation. As far as it is possible to determine, the composer's original intentions should be the foremost consideration. Only after individual opinions have merged into mutual understanding can a unified interpretation of a cadenza be presented.

CHAPTER XIII

RECITATIVES

In the recitative, or dramatic declamation, the text of the opera, cantata, oratorio, or melodrama attains primary prominence, whereas the music becomes of secondary importance. On the stage, the recitative is introduced chiefly in scenes of intense excitement, fearful suspense, or overpowering anger, as well as in passages of humor, bantering, or light-hearted gaiety. In such situations, the recitative, which bears the meaning of the text, becomes of particular import to the unraveling of the plot for which the musical accompaniment acts as support.

Clear distinction may be made between two major categories of recitatives: the *secco*-recitative, which is usually accompanied by a solo keyboard instrument, and the more elaborate dramatic recitative which requires orchestral accompaniment.

The *secco*-recitative closely resembles natural speech set to music. It is most frequently accompanied by such keyboard instruments as the Harpsichord, Organ, or Piano; orchestral accompaniment is optional. As composed by the Classical masters, the accompaniment was often notated in the form of figured bass. (See Ex. 88, 89.) Numbers written below a bass note indicated the intervals which were to be used in building up harmonic combinations. Either the conductor himself or one of the players filled in the harmonies of the figured bass on the Harpsichord. This accompaniment was frequently supplemented by one 'Cello and one Bass. In later times, masterly transcriptions of figured bass recitative accompaniments were made by such composers as Mozart, who did for Bach what later masters, including Mendelssohn, in turn did for Mozart himself. Therefore, in modern scores, transcription has completely eliminated the troublesome figured bass; instead, the full harmonic accompaniment is given.

Since the *secco*-recitative commonly consists of brief harmonic sentences punctuated by short chords, it is well adapted to animated or agitated dialogue and for the hasty communication of messages. Particularly for trivial parlance, the words are permitted free leeway to run on and on apparently without any hindrance. The interpolation of one or more chords usually supports rhythmical changes or modulations. For the most part, the *secco*-recitative endeavors to retain the natural spoken inflections of the voice for the recurring rise and fall of accented and unaccented syllables and to observe rhetorical pauses by rests.

Another type of *secco*-recitative is superimposed on an accompaniment of long sustained chords. It is sedately reserved in character and possesses a deep-rooted calmness.

The dramatic recitative, also termed *recitativo stromentato* or *recitativo accompagnato* because it is accompanied by the orchestra, is more elaborate and more rhythmical than the *secco*-recitative. Whereas the rhythmical scansion of the *secco*-recitative might be compared with the spontaneity and irregularity of free verse, the rhythm of the dramatic recitative resembles the measured and regular syllabic accentuation of blank verse, or some other poetic form.

From the time of Gluck on, the recitative has been composed almost exclusively in measured form.

In his works, Wagner greatly magnified the dramatic and declamatory potentialities of the measured recitative by a complete merging of words and music. The rhyme, alliteration, assonance, and onomatopœia of powerfully emotional verse were factors that entered into the creation of equally powerful music which became inseparable from the words. The conductor, the augmented orchestra, and the singers engaged in a glorified fusion and welding of words and music which impressively depicted the innermost motives of the characters. From this cohesion, the name "music-drama" was derived.

Melodramatic music, or incidental music to such dramas as Shakespeare's "Midsummer Night's Dream" (See Ex. 100), is in several respects similar to the secco-recitative. It is, however, more difficult to conduct, since the actors are free to take innumerable liberties, irrespective of the music. If the conductor possesses a generous amount of histrionic understanding, a major part of his problem will be solved, since he will then be able to anticipate the stage actions and conduct the orchestra accordingly. This anticipation must be grounded on a knowledge more trustworthy than mere guesswork. The conductor must have thoroughly absorbed the emotion of the dramatic situation and he must have practically memorized every word of the work he conducts.

For incidental music in dramatic radio productions, a similar dependable, detailed knowledge of the text or script must be possessed by the conductor. Whether the program requires background music for a light skit or for a Shakespearean tragedy, the tempo of the dialogue and each cue for the orchestra must be regulated and worked out with almost mathematical accuracy. At rehearsals the actors must work together with the producer, who, in turn, works with the composer, the arranger, and the conductor. These concerted efforts should lead to a successful broadcast.

Absolute mastery of the text as well as the music is needed for conducting all types of recitatives. When the word supersedes or is equal in importance to the music, the conductor must equip himself with decidedly more than a "bird's-eye-view" of the text. With only a haphazard and hastily gleaned acquaintance with the words, it will be impossible for him to produce a unified performance. The disjointed results will be a stilted and amateurish series of discrepancies utterly lacking in either dramatic or musical force. Impressive declamation will be reduced to seemingly absurd oratory. Instead, the artistically satisfying recitative should be marked by the utmost cooperation between the actor or singer and the conductor, so that not one atom of dramatic force is lost.

Similarly, the singer must master not only the solo but also the interpolated accompaniment, in order to make correct entries.

For the conductor, *following* the recitative is an utterly fallacious method. On the contrary, the conductor must be *with* the soloist, or, one might even say, *ahead* of the soloist. Every interpretative nuance must be anticipated so that, just before the word is sung or spoken, the baton is prepared for action, to bring both the word and music together simultaneously.

A current story concerns itself with an over-opulent and self-aggrandized genius of the baton who possessed the pecuniary means to engage the leading artists for soloists in his performances. Seldom were more than a few minutes' rehearsal necessary to convince the soloists that they were entrapped in a situation where only the prospect of the customary sizable check could persuade them to continue their work. On one occasion when innumerable attempts had not succeeded in combining the soprano recitative with the orchestra, the conductor tried to pass the predicament off lightly. "Don't worry; it will be all right tonight", the unperturbed conductor remarked to his very perturbed fair soloist, "I'll be sure to follow you." "Oh", she coyly smiled at him through gritted teeth, "I would so much rather go hand in hand with you, even if there is an audience to spy on us . . ."

Another similar story concerns a very gifted young operatic coach whose burning ambition was to be a conductor. After repeated requests, the impresario finally gave the young man an opportunity to conduct Gounod's "Faust". Entranced with this prospect, the novice-conductor called a full rehearsal—and began. The Prologue between Faust and Mephistopheles did not proceed too well. But since the young man was a popular favorite with the members of the company, every singer and orchestra member felt personally responsible and tried doubly hard to help him through the performance. In the Kermesse scene, his lack of baton technique made it extremely difficult for the principal singers, chorus, and orchestra to keep together. Nervousness and excitement gradually crept upon him. Then came the recitatives of Valentine, Wagner, and Siebel. The situation became unendurable, but still the headstrong young conductor remained unaware that his inexperience was responsible for this disconcerting and miserable performance. Finally, before the "Song of the Golden Calf" was reached, he lost all composure and vented his anger upon the orchestra: "Why under the sun, *etc.*, can't you follow me!" The rhetorical question was soon quietly but pointedly answered by the Third Horn player: "If you don't take care, perhaps we will!"

For the conducting of recitatives, the motions of the baton must be economical and unpedantic, in order to give the soloist the greatest amount of ease and freedom. For the measured recitative, the tempo should be so flexible as to permit *tempo rubato* liberties in accordance with the changing emotions of the text.

In free recitative, the strokes are more or less intuitively prompted by the rhythmical pulsation in the rise and fall of syllables, which are partly imitated in the musical support. Essential dramatic impulses will demand that the support fall together with the right word. The rhythmical momentum inherent in the versification guides the baton without any disconcerting jerkiness from one punctuation to the next. Between such punctuating chords there should be an unobtrusively gliding motion, giving visual expression to the feelings induced by the words.

In the case of the Classical *secco*-recitative with accompanying Harpsichord, Organ, or Piano, it is customary to omit the conducting motions entirely. Often the accompaniment is played behind the stage, as in the "Barbiere di Siviglia".

The problem of conducting-motions for the varied types of recitatives is taken up in more explicit detail in the following musical examples and diagrams:

Ex. 88a.

Excerpt from the Cantata, No. 147

"Herz und Mund und That und Leben"*   Johann Sebastian Bach

Recitative   (1685-1750)

*Breitkopf and Härtel, Leipzig, Full Score, page 208. **By permission.**

This example presents a *secco*-recitative with a figured bass performed on the Cembalo or Harpsichord, with optional 'Cello and Bass. When the figured bass, as in this case, appears in a score as the accompaniment of a vocal part, it is also termed *basso continuo* or fundamental bass, since the bass continues uninterrupted throughout the composition. This method of indicating the harmonic intervals by writing figures below the bass note was a kind of musical short-hand which was already in use a century before Palestrina and which did not become obsolete until the Romantic Period in the nineteenth century made chromatic harmonies predominant. The invention of this concise method of figured notation was a decided boon to the early ecclesiastical writers and to copyists, especially since score printing was not developed until the beginning of the sixteenth century. In the practice of Bach, Handel, Mozart, and other masters of this exquisite art, the harmonies prescribed by the composer's figures were further enhanced by means of ornate passage-work, arpeggios, melodic imitations of the solo part, contrapuntal devices, and other embellishments. A modern transcription of the above recitative from Bach's Cantata, as it would actually be performed, is presented in Example 88 (b):

Ex. 88b.

Excerpt from the Cantata, No. 147
"Herz und Mund und That und Leben"*   Johann Sebastian Bach

Recitative

*Breitkopf and Härtel, Leipzig, Vocal Score, page 16. **By permission.**

The performance of this *secco*-recitative requires hours of meticulous rehearsing with the utmost degree of cooperation between the soloist and the accompanist. When the conductor himself plays the Cembalo or Harpsichord, he retains at all times his powers of guidance, but in no way restricts the singer's freedom. As soon as the first *forte* chord has been sounded, a nod or some other visible gesture acts as a cue for the soloist to begin the recitative. The art of accompanying this recitative is principally concerned with following the word rather than the melodic line. An analysis of the sustained chords will show that the interpretative nuances in the accompaniment are dependent upon a feeling for the poetic import of the words, which give the impetus to changes in harmony.

Ex. 89a.

Recitative from Act I, Scene 1, of
"The Marriage of Figaro" (Le Nozze di Figaro)*   Wolfgang Amadeus Mozart
Recitativo

* Eulenburg 916, Full Score, pages 36-37. **By permission of Breitkopf & Härtel, Leipzig.**

The statements regarding Example 88 (*a* and *b*) also pertain to this *secco*-recitative from Mozart's "The Marriage of Figaro". No conducting motions whatsoever are needed, since the entire accompaniment consists of the figured bass chords played on a single keyboard instrument. As also in other types of accompaniment, the interpretation and the words of the singer are to be followed scrupulously.

Ex. 89b.

Recitative from Act I, Scene 1, of
"The Marriage of Figaro" (Le Nozze di Figaro)*   Wolfgang Amadeus Mozart

Recitativo

Susanna

Co - sa stai mi - su - ran - do, ca - ro il mio Fi - ga - ret - to? Io

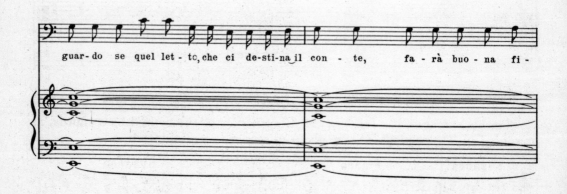

guar - do se quel let - to, che ci de - sti - na il con - te, fa - rà buo - na fi -

Susanna   Figaro

gu - ra in ques - to lo - co. In ques - ta stan - za! Cer - to, a noi la

* Breitkopf and Härtel, Leipzig, Vocal Score, page 13. By permission.

In this example, the full sustained harmonies of the figured bass chords, as presented in Example 89 (*a*), are given in modern score notation.

Ex. 90.
Recitative from "The Messiah" *
George Frederic Handel
(1685-1759)

und das Ohr des Tau-ben wird hö-ren; dann läuft der Lah-me wie ein
and the ears of the deaf un-stopped; then shall the lame man leap as a

Hirsch, und die Zun - ge des Stum-men wird sin - gen.
hart, and the tongue of the dumb shall sing.

* Eulenburg 956, page 109.

Fig. 105

In this *secco*-recitative, the original figured bass for Cembalo and String ensemble has been transcribed into modern notation. In the traditional manner of conducting this type of recitative, weight is given to the baton stroke only when the harmony of the sustained chords changes. During the sustaining of the chords, the length as well as the weight of the remaining strokes is proportionately reduced, as illustrated by Figure 105. In Example 90, strength is imparted to the down-stroke at (*a*), whereas the second, third, and fourth strokes of the first bar, as also the first and second of the following bar, are comparatively lighter and smaller baton movements. The third stroke at (*b*) gathers force since it introduces a new sustained harmony. Similarly, both the preparatory movement and the down-stroke at (*c*) are forceful. A point for special observation is the end of the recitative at (*d*) where the distinct delivery of the text is in danger of being overpowered by the authentic cadence for the instruments. In order to avoid obscuring the articulation, it has become customary in all Classical musical literature, particularly in Handel's works, to perform the punctuating chords immediately after the last word of the recitative.   After the first pulsation of the last bar, the effect of two strong rhythmical pulsations is produced by a down-stroke at (*e*) and the succeeding end-stroke.

Ex. 91.
Recitative from "The Messiah"*   George Frederic Handel

*Eulenburg 956, page 253.

The procedure in conducting this recitative is precisely the same as that outlined for the preceding excerpt from the "Messiah" (Example 90).   The same traditional principles are also to be observed in producing an effective closing cadence.

Ex. 92.
Recitative from "L'Elisir d'amore"*   Gaetano Donizetti

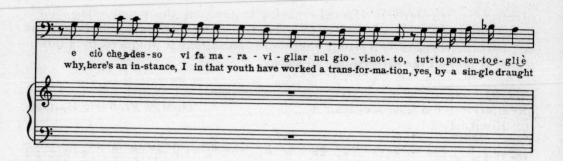

e ciò che a-des-so   vi fa ma - ra - vi - gliar nel gio - vi-not- to, tut-to por-ten-to e- glie
why, here's an in-stance, I in that youth have worked a trans-for-ma-tion, yes, by a sin-gle draught

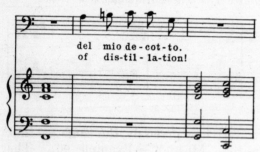

del   mio de - cot - to.
of   dis-til - la-tion!

✻ Boosey & Co., Vocal Score, page 246.

Fig. 106

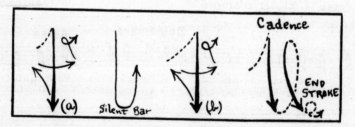

The first chord (*a*) announces the key's tonality, and is then released by an appropriate motion of the left hand. The release acts as a cue to the singer to begin the recitative. After a small light stroke for the silent measure, a down-stroke and release are made at (*b*), similar to the procedure at (*a*). For each following silent measure, a single light down-stroke is in order, whereas the sustained chords require emphatic strokes. The two final chords are practically similar to those closing the recitatives in Examples 90 and 91. However, even though the chords in this case are written out as whole-notes, the effect will be heightened if they are played like two quarter-notes. No actual time-signature has been indicated by the composer, in order to permit the greatest amount of freedom in the performance of this recitative.

Ex. 93.

Recitative from "Il Barbiere di Siviglia" *

Gioachino Rossini
(1792-1862)

Recitativo

Figaro

(a)
Ah, ah! che bel - la vi - ta! Fa - ti - car po - co, di - ver - tir - si as -
Yes, yes, this life is glo - rious! Not much to do, and plen - ty of a -

Strings

sa - i, e in tas - ca sem - pre a - ver qual-che do - blo - ne. Gran frut - to del - la mia ri - pu - ta -
muse-ment, and al - ways a doub - loon with - in my pock - et! The fruit of my ex - alt - ed rep - u -

(b)

zio - ne. Ec - co qua: sen - za Fi - ga - ro non si ac - ca - sa in Si -
ta - tion. It is thus: with - out Fi - ga - ro, not a girl in all

(c)

vi - glia u - na ra - gaz - za; a me la ve - do - vel - la ri - cor - re pel ma - ri - to:
Se - ville can find a hus - band; to me the gen - tle wid - ow turns her ap - peal - ing glan - ces;

* G. Schirmer, Inc., Vocal Score, page 41.

Fig. 107

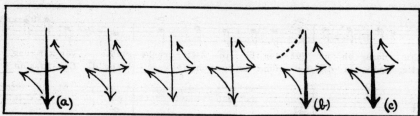

Even though the sustained note (*a*) beginning the accompaniment is to be prolonged over four bars, its actual duration is very short. Only the down-stroke in the first bar should be strong. The other strokes will be a series of almost inconspicuous movements indicating the passage of time. The baton never becomes stationary, but its motion is kept alive by the vivacity of this recitative. When the harmonic foundation is altered in the 5th and 6th bars (*b* and *c*), strength should again enter both the preparatory movements and the down-strokes. It is self-evident that the absence of all ostentatious conducting permits the soloist the widest range of *tempo rubato* freedom.

Ex. 94.
Recitative from "Lohengrin" *

Richard Wagner

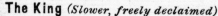

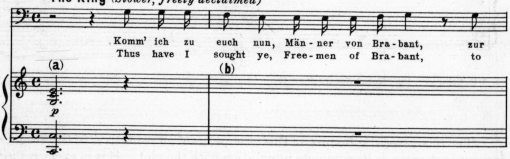

* G. Schirmer, Inc., Vocal Score, page 10.

The characteristic feature of this excerpt, as of all recitatives in the Wagnerian music-dramas, is its complete integration with the plot. It is in every respect an unforced and natural outgrowth of the dramatic situation. As already indicated on Page 90, the words of this free declamation, the music, and the stage action are so closely coordinated and welded together that there is never an instant of dissociation or interruption in the continuity of the work as an artistic whole.

The portion of the King's declamation given in the above example is written in measured rhythm, for which a $\frac{4}{4}$ conducting scheme is applicable. The singer does not begin the recitative until the third pulsation of the first chord (*a*) in the String accompaniment has been released. The silent bar (*b*) is then conducted with a light down-stroke whose movement continues upward into a preparatory stroke to introduce the next chord at (*c*). In the remaining bars, as in the preceding examples of recitatives, added weight is given to the baton stroke only when harmonic changes occur in the accompanying chords.

Ex. 95.

Recitative from "Lohengrin"*   Richard Wagner

Poco allegro

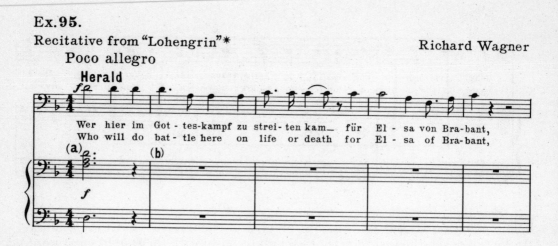

Wer hier im Got - tes-kampf zu strei - ten kam_ für El - sa von Bra-bant,
Who will do bat - tle here on life or death for El - sa of Bra-bant,

der tre - te vor!   Der tre - te vor!
let him ap - pear!   Let him ap-pear!

Ohn'   Ant - wort ist der   Ruf   ver - hallt! Ge-wahrt
No   cham-pion to the   call   comes forth! Ye see

*G. Schirmer, Inc., Vocal Score, page 38.

Fig. 108

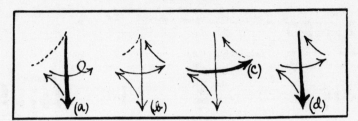

For this dramatic recitative in measured form, the conducting strokes follow out a $\frac{4}{4}$ pattern. A vigorous preparatory movement and then a downstroke (a) attack the first *forte* chord simultaneously with the Herald's first word. During the ensuing silent measures, while the Herald calls upon a champion, the strokes of the $\frac{4}{4}$ diagram may be continued, but with such slightness of movement that they serve merely as aids to those instrumentalists who mentally count bars for accurate entries. With a particularly well-trained orchestra, a single down-stroke suffices for each silent measure, without following through the second, third, and fourth strokes of the diagram. However, at (c), (d), (e), and the remaining measures in this excerpt, it is evident that the full conducting pattern must be used. Special power should mark the stroke for the short chords, while the rests are conducted with comparatively insignificant movements. Immediately after the Herald's call, a feeling of tense waiting and ominous dramatic suspense pervades the atmosphere. To give the entry-cue for the Chorus's subdued comment, the conductor not only looks up from the score, but also increases the elevation of the baton strokes, as an additional device for assuring the simultaneous entry of voices in the Chorus.

Ex. 96.
Recitative from "Elijah"*   Felix Mendelssohn

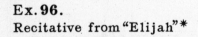

*G. Schirmer, Inc., page 70.

In this recitative, the Prophet's scathing derision lashes the idol-worshipers who call upon Baal, the false God.   The dramatic power of the text is augmented by the impassioned accompaniment, music which is fraught with scorn and vehement irony.

The chorus's cadence, closing the recitative previous to the beginning of this excerpt, establishes the tonality for the soloist, who then begins independently and sets the tempo with the first words of the text, *"Rufet lauter!"*   Throughout this measured recitative, the conductor follows out a ⁴⁄₄ scheme with strong and emphatic strokes for the *sforzando* and *forte* chords.

Ex. 97.
Recitative from "Aïda"*

Giuseppe Verdi
(1813-1901)

* G. Schirmer, Inc., Vocal Score, page 175.   International copyright by G. Ricordi & Co., Milan; used by permission.

Fig. 109

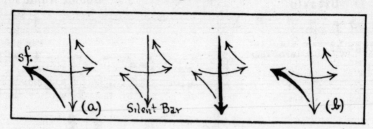

This recitative is begun by the voice alone and is then supported by an accompaniment designed to intensify the fervor of Radames's invocation to the royal mercy. It is advisable to base the conducting motions on a $\frac{4}{4}$ diagram with emphasis on these strokes marking the chords. At (a) the rest is a light stroke, followed by a *sforzando* accent on the chord. A special point for strategic conducting is (b) where an impulsive down-stroke falls paradoxically on the rest and rebounds into the next strong stroke for the two brief chords. The dynamic accentuation in this recitative is the conductor's major problem.

Ex. 98.
Recitative from "Don Giovanni"*   Wolfgang Amadeus Mozart

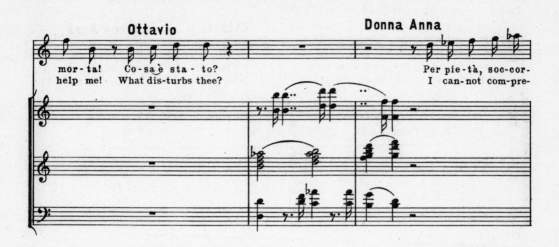

Ottavio **Donna Anna**

mor-ta! Co-sa è sta - to? Per pie-tà, soc-cor-
help me! What dis-turbs thee? I can-not com-pre-

Ottavio **Donna Anna**

re - te-mi! Mio be - ne, fa - te co - rag-gio! O De - i!
hend it yet! My dear-est, say, what hath hap-pen'd? Oh Heav-en!

O De - i! Quegli è il car-
Oh Heav-en! That was the

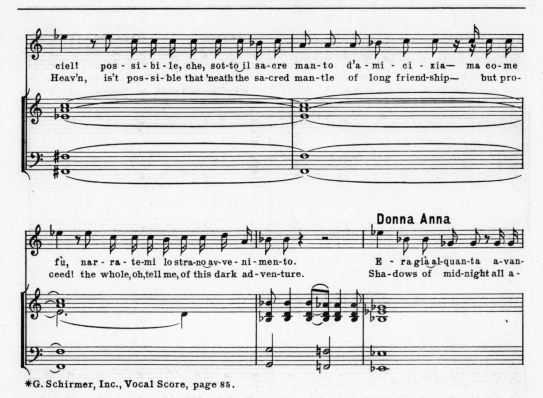

*G. Schirmer, Inc., Vocal Score, page 85.

The accompaniment for this recitative is particularly descriptive of the dramatic situation. A suggestion of tragic conflict lies in the opening tones for 'Cello and Bass, followed an instant later by Wood-wind, Horns, and Trumpets, and a veritable outcry from the Violins. Donna Anna cries out for the assistance of Ottavio. Her mental anguish at suddenly discovering the identity of her father's murderer, the friend of Ottavio, is reflected in the perturbed snatches of the accompaniment. The intricate rhythmical construction of these dramatically motivated fragments calls for conducting motions throughout the excerpt. At the same time, the *parlando* of the singers should not be restricted.

Ex. 99.
Recitative from "Carmen"*   Georges Bizet

*G. Schirmer, Inc., Vocal Score, page 187.

In this recitative, the conductor encounters an extremely flexible *tempo rubato*, adapted to the interplay of changing moods. Flippancy, intense adoration, deliberate casualness, hurt pride, and jealousy, all are contained in varied tempos within the space of a few measures.

At (a), the chord is impulsively attacked on the second stroke of a $\frac{4}{4}$ scheme. In the next three measures the same type of impulsive stroke is repeated. At (b), the accompaniment may linger with *Don José's "je t'adore";* but a moment later, the *allegro* passage (c) quickly changes the mood. At (d), the conductor must be on the alert to give the necessary cue for the sustained *A* of the Horns.

Ex. 100

Incidental Music to "A Midsummer Night's Dream"*   Felix Mendelssohn

Dialógue

Bottom: Are we all met?

*   *   *

Quince: And so everyone according to his cue.

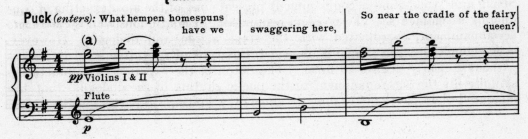

* Novello & Co., London, Vocal Score, page 50.

This outstanding example of the melodramatic recitative with incidental String and Wood-wind accompaniment presents one of the most exacting of conducting assignments. The problem centers almost continuously on *tempo rubato* accompaniment, coordinated with the stage action and dialogue. However, even though no strict tempo is observed, this type of recitative is by no means without a clearly delineated form. The baton of the experienced conductor so skilfully fits the accompaniment to the poetic rhythm of the dialogue, that the measured blank verse meter directly affects the rhythmical pattern of the music.

This pattern is particularly evident in the motive for Flute from (*a*) to (*b*), which is measure-for-measure rhythmically indentical with the Bassoon's and Ophicleide's motive from (*d*) to (*e*). During the *fermata* on the rest at (*b*), the conductor mentally follows the dialogue without accompaniment in order to give the preparatory stroke for the next orchestral entry (*c*). Throughout this excerpt from a woodland fantasy, the *pianissimo tremolo* for Strings retains a lightness descriptive of the whirring of crickets and the stirrings of tiny forest creatures.

The conducting or accompanying of each of the preceding examples of recitatives (Ex. 88–100) requires great adeptness in the use of *tempo rubato*, one of the most severe tests of the good conductor. Just as in the case of the cadenza, both soloist and conductor will require many rehearsals, privately and with orchestra, before the recitative and the accompaniment are shaped into a well-integrated musical performance.

CONCLUSION

The foregoing chapters have equipped the student with a practical knowledge of baton technique, so that he will be able to cope intelligently with the technicalities of conducting problems arising in the course of his experience. He will also have gained sufficient insight into the symbols of the baton's language to reach out toward interpretative eloquence.

Interpretation is in a wide sense a synonym for imagination. The technical control of an instrument or of an orchestra is by no means sufficient in itself to impart life to a musical work. Imagination, joined with culture, endows the conductor with the gift of feeling deeply the emotion of the composer's ideas and of transmitting it into musical tone.

The conductor's powers of interpretation must be grounded not only in his imagination, but also in positive knowledge. An analysis of the differences in old and new styles of composition and of the ways to adapt conducting procedures to them is absolutely essential. In *THE LANGUAGE OF THE BATON—BOOK TWO*, the author aims to present an opportunity for further exploration into interpretative problems, acoustics and seating arrangements, ear-training, conducting methods for marches, dances, and symphonic forms, instrumentation problems, specific chorus, band, and radio problems, and other significant phases of conducting.

INDEX OF
COMPOSERS AND MUSICAL EXAMPLES

GENERAL INDEX